MEASURE WHAT
MATTERS

Online Tools For Understanding
Customers, Social Media, Engagement,
and Key Relationships

KATIE DELAHAYE PAINE
WILLIAM T. PAARLBERG, EDITOR

WILEY

John Wiley & Sons, Inc.

Published by John Wiley & Sons, Inc., Hoboken, New Jersey.
Published simultaneously in Canada.

For general information on our other products and services or for technical support, please contact our Customer Care Department within the United States at (800) 762-2974, outside the United States at (317) 572-3993 or fax (317) 572-4002.

Wiley also publishes its books in a variety of electronic formats. Some content that appears in print may not be available in electronic books. For more information about Wiley products, visit our web site at www.wiley.com.

Library of Congress Cataloging-in-Publication Data:

Delahaye Paine, Katie, 1952–
    Measure what matters : online tools for understanding customers, social media,
        engagement, and key relationships / Katie Paine.
            p. cm.
        Includes bibliographical references and index.
        ISBN 978-0-470-92010-7 (hardback) ISBN 978-1-118-01630-5 (ebk);
        ISBN 978-1-118-01631-2 (ebk); ISBN 978-1-118-01632-9 (ebk)
    1. Customer services—Research.   2. Social media—Research.   3. Measurement.
    I. Title.
    HF5415.5.P34 2011
    659.20285′4678–dc22   2010043310

Printed in the United States of America.

10 9 8 7 6 5 4 3 2 1

I dedicate this one to my father, Ralph D. Paine, for teaching me to write what I know. To my lifelong editors Geoffrey Precourt, who taught me how to write; Charlie O'Brien, who taught me how to make what I write interesting; and William Teunis Paarlberg, who may be the only person who can finish my sentences and make what I'm trying to say both logical and interesting. And to Shel Israel who taught me how to convince skeptics that measurement is important and relevant. —KDP

CONTENTS

Chapter 2
How to Get Started   19

Chapter 3
Seven Steps to the Perfect Measurement Program:
How to Prove Your Results and Use Your Results
to Improve   33

Part 2
HOW TO MEASURE WHAT PEOPLE ARE SAYING ABOUT YOU ONLINE AND OFF

Chapter 5
How to Measure Marketing, Public Relations, and Advertising in a Social Media World   69

FOREWORD

Now here is a book that is far more than its predecessor. In *Measure What Matters*, author Katie Delahaye Paine and editor William T. Paarlberg revitalize rather than merely revise the curriculum of the University of Measurement as originally presented in *Measuring Public Relationships*. Much of that original work is here: both the theory and the nitty-gritty of measurement, especially the measurement of relationships. What is new is an emphasis on social media in a business context.

Readers will still appreciate the appendix of resources that include books on research and questionnaire items measuring qualities and types of relationships. We still benefit from Katie's rich experience—brilliantly written anecdotes, all. Her sidebars of case studies, such as the campaign for SeaWorld that illustrates the role of social media in reaching key influencers, help bring home the solid principles on which this book is based. The figures, too, help confirm the assertions in the text.

The writing here, as previously, is cogent and transparent. Katie makes the arcane world of measurement both understandable and interesting. In other words, readers not only will "get it," they'll want to get *into* it, into the myriad decisions that must be made even before a project is evaluated. The intriguing subheads contribute to the excitement of what has been, for many people, a dull subject. Who wouldn't want to read more when confronted with "If You Have No Budget at All," "You're Not in Control—and Never Have Been," or "BS Is More Damaging than Lies."

Yes, Katie is clever . . . and she's also wise. Take, for just one example, the section headed "A Word on Measuring ROI." Given all the *Sturm und Drang* that typically accompany this concept, we especially appreciated the provision of five ways to determine the return, approaches that extend well beyond sales or revenue to include, for example, social capital. She also takes care to explain how to come up with the resources necessary to conduct such evaluation, a discussion that characterized the earlier text as well.

One difference here though, as reflected in the title of the new book, is the emphasis on measurement as a *business tool*. This shift is consistent with today's aspiration and inclusion of public relations people in the C-suite.

The organization of this text, by stakeholders, remains appropriate. After all, relationships with different groups of publics remain the *raison d'être* of public relations. Along the way, Katie writes with confidence and candor. As a result, she helps create the very kind of relationship with readers that she urges them to measure with their publics—a relationship born of trust. For just one example, how many professional communicators do you know—especially among those who earn a living doing research—who remind you that less can be more when conducting a survey? As Katie puts it: "You can probably get most of the information you need from talking to 250 people . . . [s]o don't get talked into surveying thousands if you don't really need to." Good advice, but rare in a world where commercial firms may charge by the numbers—and thus appropriate to retain in the new version of the book. Katie goes on to explain that it's possible to survey a mere 500 people and get a representative sample of the whole population of the United States.

The book speaks to novices and veterans of the world of measurement. It ends with a glossary of relevant terms, from the controversial—such as AVEs—to the more straightforward—such as "trend analysis."

Throughout, Katie emphasizes the importance of measuring *relationships* created and nurtured via digital media. In this way alone, she sets her book apart from many others—those that focus on media hits, for example, or strategic messaging. She clearly differentiates among measuring outputs, outtakes, and outcomes. She proceeds from one strategic public to another, not assuming that one system of measurement fits all. So she describes how to measure relationships with the community, opinion leaders, employees, members, volunteers, investors, partners, the media, and sales reps. She teases out what is unique about evaluating relationships in times of crisis and through blogs and other new media. She explains how to plan and budget.

Katie does all this through both words and numbers—exactly as a competent research report would be prepared. She infuses this new look at measurement with her solid grasp of all the social media. By emphasizing measurement as a tool for businesspeople rather than public relations people alone, she extends the scope of *Measure What Matters*. "Scope" may be inadequate here; perhaps we should characterize the reach of this guide to measurement as an "enormous sweep."

In any case, Katie Paine has walked the walk that so many of our colleagues merely talk about. The typical book on research, like too many researchers, overpromises and underdelivers. Readers, anxious to know more and to do better, approach these books with optimism but leave in frustration at the level of the text or its inadequate explication. At the very least, their minds feel chloroformed by the language.

By contrast, here we have a book that is a vivid, engaging, accessible, and wise reflection of what Katie does and all she knows. It's nifty stuff and well worth knowing.

Larissa A. Grunig
James E. Grunig
Professors Emeriti
Department of Communication
University of Maryland

PREFACE

"We talk about the quality of product and service. What about the quality of our relationships, and the quality of our communications, and the quality of our promises to each other?"

—Max De Pree

I am amazed at the continuing significance of the quotation above: What about the quality of our relationships? It is an essential and perennial question that lies at the heart of our social and business lives. Many of the examples of corporate relationships that I used in my book *Measuring Public Relationships* are included in this new book as well, and all of them ring just as true today as they did then. Now, just as then, measuring what matters means measuring relationships.

The difference is, of course, that everything in our world has changed. In just a few short years the social media phenomenon has radically shifted our political, social, and—especially—corporate landscape. Traditional media outlets are closing daily. Marketing is moving dollars out of traditional advertising and into social media strategies at a breakneck pace. And the illusion of control that corporate communications once thought it had over its messages and stakeholders has vanished forever in a sea of tweets, updates, and blog posts.

Success, timing, media, and PR have all been redefined by social media. Success can no longer be measured in terms of reach or frequency, since neither is particularly easy to determine in this new space. Success must now be defined in terms of outcomes: What do you want your program to do for the organization?

Timing has been changed forever by the demise of deadlines. It used to be that you had at least until 5 P.M. to make the evening news with a comment. Now, if that comment isn't posted on Twitter within an hour or so, people will begin to accuse you of ducking the issue. In the social media world, two or three hours may be all you have to get your story straight.

The definitions and boundaries between different forms of media are another moving target. It used to be that National Public Radio was radio, but now that more and more people are getting their news from the NPR website, that site must be constantly fed with music, pictures, and video. So do you classify that as "radio" or as "online news?" (Hint: It's the latter.)

And when did we ever think of local TV stations as a place for still photographs? But today they are: During any major weather crisis, visitors to TV websites are invited to post their storm pictures for the world to see. In some ways we are all now photojournalists.

The notion that a PR person is someone who has to deal only with the press is just as antiquated. A good PR person is focused on his or her relationships—be they with the local media, national bloggers, employees, or community organizers.

And so we are back to the big point here: relationships. All transactions conducted today—from buying a printer, to donating to a cause, to protesting a local initiative—are still (and, I would argue, always will be) driven by relationships. The difference is that a decade ago we talked primarily about relationships between corporations and their stakeholders. Now the relationship is just as likely to be between two individuals on your Facebook page. Actually, make that millions of individuals on millions of Facebook pages. And without knowing how to measure those millions of relationships, you are more likely than ever to be lost in a sea of data, words, and reactions.

Over more than two decades I've measured communications programs for hundreds of organizations. I've figured out how to measure
successes in many, many shapes and forms: public relations, media relations, employee communications, events, sponsorships, trade shows,
and academia. And I can honestly say that no one has brought me
a communications program that I could not develop measurement
for. I actually started measuring social media back in 1996, when it
was known as "consumer-generated media" and my company was
tracking the sentiment of newsgroup mentions regarding computer
printers. Through all those years and all those programs, the one
common denominator has been relationships—lots of different types
of relationships with lots of different constituencies.

I am convinced that the key to understanding corporate reputation is measuring the relationships that it is based on. Whether you
work for a Fortune 500 international powerhouse or run a local nonprofit, you share a common interest in the relationships you have
with your constituencies. Building, managing, and measuring those
relationships are fundamental to your success and the success of your
organization.

As our world has become more electronic and, in many ways,
less personal, the importance of those relationships has increased.
Our new and efficient communication technologies make relationships easier to initiate but sometimes operate to the detriment of
relationships—both interpersonal and organizational. And for some
organizations, understanding how to measure and better manage their
relationships is becoming a matter of survival. If you can measure your
relationships you can improve them, and so improve your communications effectiveness and overall performance.

This book has grown from my experience in designing and implementing measurement systems. It is based on hundreds of actual
stories about how organizations have used measurement to improve
their reputations, strengthen their bottom lines, and improve effi-
ciencies all around. The following pages provide you with tools,

tips, techniques, and experiences that illustrate how to measure your success, and specifically the success of your relationships. This is a book that all professional communicators can use—whether they work for Procter & Gamble or for a small, local nonprofit—to improve their work and the organizations they work for.

Here's wishing you nearly immeasurable amounts of success.

Katie Delahaye Paine

PART 1

NOT YOUR FATHER'S RULER

CHAPTER 1

You Can Now Measure Everything, but You Won't Survive Without the Metrics that Matter to Your Business

"What is wanted is not the will to believe, but the will to find out, which is the exact opposite."

—Bertrand Russell

Until recently, the attitude toward measurement in business has been: "It's too expensive and too complicated and really only applicable for major corporations." In the past decade, however, a confluence of circumstances has pushed measurement and metrics onto the priority lists of businesspeople everywhere.

First there was the Internet explosion. The Internet, and specifically social media, has been adopted by businesses worldwide in record-breaking time. It took 89 years for the telephone to reach the level of household penetration that Facebook reached in just five.

As consumers increasingly research and purchase goods online, their behaviors, thoughts, and opinions have become easier to track and measure. At the same time, the proliferation of listening, analysis, and reporting tools has made such metrics affordable and accessible to every organization, from nonprofits to go-fast Internet start-ups.

3

Then there is the current global recession. In these hard times most every business is taking a hard look at what strategies, programs, and communications are working and not working. Today, if you're in business and want to survive, you will need to continuously measure and improve your processes and programs. Whether or not *you* are measuring, your *competition* very likely is—and as a result probably knows more about your business than you do.

This book will do much more than just teach you how to measure. It will teach you how to measure what you need to make the decisions that are crucial to your business. It used to be that "he or she with the most data wins." But today nothing is cheaper and easier to come by than data—especially useless data. It's having the *right* data that counts.

While every program is different, all organizations have a core set of key publics with whom they need to build relationships, collectively known as the *stakeholders*. These include, among others: the media, employees, customers, distributors or sales force, the local community, industry influencers, financial analysts, and elected officials. Each stakeholder group requires slightly different measurement tools and slightly different metrics. That's why this book is organized around the stakeholders—each with its own chapter and its own procedures and advice. This book shows you how to measure business relationships with just about any key public that your job involves.

SOCIAL MEDIA ISN'T ABOUT MEDIA, IT'S ABOUT THE COMMUNITY IN WHICH YOU DO BUSINESS

Most of what I advocate in this book wouldn't be possible or necessary without social media. We talk about social media as a shiny new object, as if it's some sort of new toy for business. In fact, social media has changed everything important to your business. From marketing and sales to employee and financial management, the social media revolution has forced all of us to rethink how we approach business, our marketplaces, and our customers.

Today, customers talk to and trust each other more than they do companies. They choose how they spend their time and money based on recommendations from people with similar tastes and profiles. They trust, and therefore prefer to do business with, companies that are open, honest, and authentic. Companies with which they have good relationships are more likely to be forgiven when they make a mistake. Thus, companies that listen carefully to their customers and respond to their needs will survive and prosper. Those who don't will be gone.

In order to succeed in this new era of easy and frequent conversations, it is critical that you continuously listen to and evaluate what your market is saying about you. Companies that do can promote themselves more efficiently, innovate more effectively, and operate more profitably.

MEASUREMENT IS SO MUCH MORE THAN COUNTING

Before we get into the how-to's of measurement we need to be clear on our definitions. Everyone in business already has some form of accounting in place. All business owners know how to count inventory, the number of ads they place, or the number of stories in which they are mentioned. They count their customers, their sales, and generally count their profits.

But counting is very different from measurement.

Counting just adds things up and gets a total. *Measurement* takes those totals, analyzes what they mean, and uses that meaning to improve business practices. Measurement of your processes and results—where you spend your time and money and what you get out of it—provides the data necessary to make sound decisions. It helps you set priorities, allocate resources, and make choices. Without it, hunches and gut feelings prevail. Without it, mistakes get made and no one learns from them.

WHAT REALLY MATTERS TO YOUR BUSINESS?

Only a handful of businesses—those that prosper, grow, and continuously improve—measure what matters. Most organizations, when asked what really matters to their business, would probably say, "my customers," or "my employees." And they'd be partially correct. But it's not the *number* of customers and employees that matters, it's the *relationships* that your organization has with them that matters.

Good relationships lead to profits. With good relationships, prospects become customers and customers become loyal advocates for your company. Thanks to good relationships, employees stay, learn, grow, and contribute to their organizations. Poor relationships result in more expensive operations, fewer sales, less customer loyalty, more churn, higher legal fees, higher turnover rates, more expensive recruiting costs, and, ultimately, disadvantage in the marketplace.

In public relations, if you establish good relationships with reporters, bloggers, editors, and other key influencers, they'll trust your word, cut you slack in a crisis, and turn to you for your thoughts and opinions. A lack of good relationships with the media leads to crises escalating, omission from key stories, and less inclusion of your point of view in stories.

So what really matters is your relationships and the aggregated outcome of those relationships: your reputation. Today, if you're not measuring the health of your relationships, you won't be in business for very long. This book tells you how to measure those relationships and what to do with the data once you have it.

WHY MEASURE AT ALL?

When budgets are flush, there's a popular misconception that it doesn't much matter how you measure results, as long as there is a perfunctory number that shows up for your department every so often. But times aren't always flush. And the bean counters and stakeholders are getting more demanding. Even when profits are rising, measurement saves time and money.

The spectacular proliferation of social media—from Twitter to Facebook to YouTube and beyond—means the average businessperson is faced with a bewildering array of opportunities and obstacles. It's a new and rapidly changing world out there, and the most productive way to run your business is not obvious. The prudent and productive approach is to measure the results of all your efforts in a consistent manner and compare the results against a clearly articulated and predefined set of goals.

When I entered the field of corporate communications it was by way of journalism, and I had little practical knowledge of communications tactics and strategies. So I asked a lot of questions, such as, "Where do we get the most bang for the buck?" and "Which strategy results in the cheapest cost per message communicated?" At the time, no one had the answers at their fingertips, so I developed systems to get the data. And for more than two decades I have been refining those systems and developing new ones. You will read about them in detail in the following chapters.

Along the way I learned that measuring your success is not just another buzzword that follows Six Sigma, TQM, and paradigm shifts. It is a key strategic tool that helps you better manage your resources, your department, and your career. No matter what type or size of organization you are in, there are half a dozen advantages to setting up a measurement program. Here they are:

Data-Driven Decision Making Saves Time and Money

Making decisions based on data saves time and boosts your credibility. When faced with tough decisions, you'll seldom find boards of directors or CEOs relying on hunches or gut instinct. Chances are any decisions made at the highest levels will be made following extensive research.

So why should other business decisions be any different? How credible would your CFO be if he got up in front of the board and said, "I know we're making money because I see the checks coming in"? Just as the CFO relies on accounting data to give advice and make recommendations on financial issues, you need other data to decide where, when, and how to allocate resources in other departments, including HR, marketing, public affairs, communications, and sales support.

It Helps Allocate Budget and Staff

I once used a competitive media analysis to indicate the need for PR staff for a major semiconductor company. We analyzed this client's presence in key media and compared it to that of three competitors to determine who was earning the greatest share of ink. As it happened, over a two-year period there was very little difference between the competitors, with the four organizations equally matched in coverage each month. But at a certain point the client's results took a dive; all of a sudden its share of ink in the key trade media dropped to about two percent.

I presented the results and asked the audience, which included several managers, what had happened. The answer was: "That was when we reorganized and eliminated our PR effort." I replied by demonstrating that, in the months following the reorganization, the market had had about *nine times* more opportunities to see news about the competition's products than their own. That seemed to do the trick—the last time I was in touch, the PR staff had grown to about 10 people and their budget was increasing every year.

Gain a Better Understanding of the Competition

Your business or organization is always competing for something: sales, donations, search ranking results, share of conversations, share of wallet, or share of voice. So you need to know how you stack up against your peers and rivals. Measurement gives you insight into competitive strengths and weaknesses.

Strategic Planning

Deciding how to best allocate resources is arguably the most important responsibility of any manager. But without data you are forced to rely on gut instinct. And as accurate as your gut may be, it doesn't translate very well into numbers. What you need is data—data you can rely on to guide your decisions and to improve your programs.

Measurement Gets Everyone to Agree on a Desired Outcome

You can't decide what form your measurement program is going to take without an agreed upon set of goals. This alone may be the best reason to start measuring. Putting everyone in a room and getting agreement on what a program is designed to achieve eliminates countless hours of blaming and bickering later if the project doesn't work.

This is especially true with social media. Too often people will complain that marketing dollars spent on social media are "unmeasurable," when, in fact, the real reason metrics don't exist is that no one ever articulated just what the social media program was designed to do. And, "getting our feet wet in social media" is not a measurable goal—unless you're a duck.

Measurement Reveals Strengths and Weaknesses

Measurement isn't something you should do because you're forced to. It should be approached as an essential strategic tool to more effectively run your business. Deciding how to allocate the necessary resources and staff is easier if you know exactly what works and what doesn't, especially when it comes to social media.

One of my first experiences with measurement was at Lotus Development (now IBM Software). I was nearing the end of my first year there and wanted to determine what had worked and what hadn't. My primary role was to insure the successful communication of key messages to the target audience. So we gathered the 2,400 or so articles that mentioned Lotus during the previous year and analyzed each one to determine whether it left a reader more or less likely to purchase Lotus software, and whether it contained one or more of the key messages our company was trying to communicate about itself. To do the analysis I hired 20-something college students who were in the market for software. I gave them careful instructions on how to read and analyze each article to determine if it left them more or less likely to buy Lotus software.

The results were very revealing. The $350,000 launch (with a major cocktail party) of a word processing product generated plenty of coverage, but very few of those articles contained our key messages. In fact, a $15,000 press tour was much more effective at getting key messages to our target audiences. The metric we used to measure success was cost per message communicated (CPMC), and the press tour delivered a CPMC of $.02 compared to the party's CPMC of $1.50. (See Figure 1.1.) Based on this data, we immediately cut the planned $150,000 party out of the next product launch plan.

Even more revealing was our success in penetrating new markets. We were targeting software buyers with a product that required us to reach an entirely new audience that relied upon a distinct group of industry trade magazines. When we analyzed the results, we realized that this new group of journalists had not responded well to our pitch, and, in fact, their stories were only half as likely to contain key messages as was typical. I called a few of these journalists and tracked down the source of their problem, which turned out to be a member of my staff who wasn't responding in a timely manner. Through proper coaching I was ultimately able to repair the relationship.

Figure 1.1
Media analysis is one way to demonstrate
what works and what doesn't.

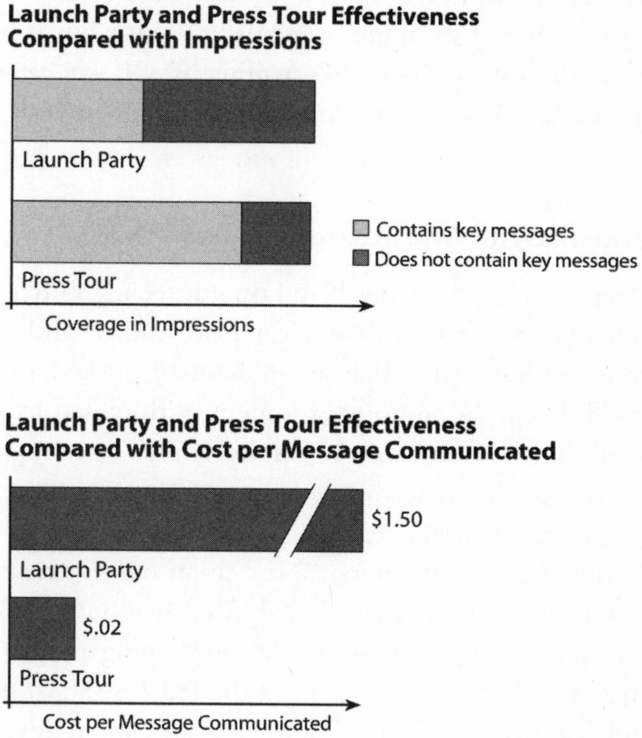

Launch Party and Press Tour Effectiveness
Compared with Impressions

Launch Party

Press Tour

Coverage in Impressions

☐ Contains key messages
■ Does not contain key messages

Launch Party and Press Tour Effectiveness
Compared with Cost per Message Communicated

$1.50

Launch Party

$.02

Press Tour

Cost per Message Communicated

Another example involves a client who had us compare the results of a press tour with those of a press conference to determine which was more effective. The results varied little in terms of quantity of coverage. In terms of *quality*, however, the press tour received nearly twice as much positive press and communicated almost twice as many messages, all for a fraction of the cost of the press conference.

Here's an example from the nonprofit world. In 2009, my company compared two programs undertaken by the USO. In one, newly elected President Obama stuffed Care packages on the White House lawn, and in another *The Colbert Report* visited Baghdad. Our metrics showed that the Colbert event generated about 10 times more publicity, but both events generated almost identical amounts of online donations, and at vastly different costs. The Obama event wasn't nearly as expensive or as interesting to the media, but it sent out a very effective message to the USO's mailing list: "If you can't be there to support the USO in person, donate online."

Measurement Gives You Reasons to Say "No"

All too often, making decisions based on gut feeling rather than data leads to overworked staff with unclear priorities. If and when you are presented with demands that seem ill-timed, rushed, or just plain unwise, there is simply no good argument with which to say "No." However, if you have data on the results of previous programs, you frequently gain the leverage you need to turn down requests that will be a waste of time or resources.

One of my clients took saying "No" to an entirely new level. At the time she was a lowly researcher, but each month she'd look at her report and highlight all the worst performing programs. She'd take the data to her boss and point out the failures. She'd then move budget and resources out of the failing programs and redirect them to those that were working. In short order the department was operating so effectively that she was promoted to vice president.

DISPELLING THE MYTHS OF MEASUREMENT

So if measurement is all that valuable and important, why isn't everyone already doing it? There are a number of bona fide reasons—lack of knowledge, lack of time, lack of a clear strategy—but most of the so-called reasons people give stem from a few commonly held myths about measurement.

Myth #1: Measurement = Punishment

Measurement is too often seen as a way to check up on people or a department and thus is too often used to justify the existence of a program or budget. People shy away from accountability, fearing that it will reveal flaws and weaknesses in the organization. However, in two decades in this business I have never seen anyone punished for being more accountable. No one I've worked with has ever been punished for showing how to make a program more efficient or for having clear and quantifiable ways to figure out what works or what doesn't. In fact, most people who institute measurement programs find that they get more promotions, bigger raises, and increased budgets because of their ability to identify strengths and weaknesses and allocate resources more intelligently.

A corollary to the Measurement = Punishment myth is, "I'm afraid I'll get bad news." Too many people are afraid of projects being cancelled because they aren't working or that they will hear unpleasant things from the stakeholders. The truth is: If something isn't working, it's wasting money and resources. So why would you want to continue it? And if people are saying bad things about your organization, they'll keep on saying them anyway, even if you're not listening and participating in the conversation.

Myth #2: Measurement Will Only Create More Work for Me

In the overall scheme of things, measurement seems to many of us just one more thing in a long list of high-priority items. Too often it gets dropped to the bottom of the list because it seems like too much work. The reality is that once a measurement system is in place, it actually makes everything else much easier. Data at your fingertips helps you to better direct the resources you have, ensuring that they are having maximum impact. Data at your disposal means less time debating the merits of one tactic over another. Gut feelings can always be second-guessed, but data is much harder to argue with.

Myth #3: Measurement Is Expensive

The number one reason that people give for not measuring is that they can't afford it. The truth is, you cannot afford *not* to measure. Without measurement, you have no way of knowing if you are spending your budget effectively. A measurement system frequently pays for itself because it inevitably leads to increased efficiency.

One international client of ours called its PR agencies together and showed them the results of our $10,000 benchmark study of their PR. Based on those results, the agencies were given concise new objectives for directing specific messages to specific audiences. Six months later, communication of the company's key messages had risen by 245 percent *and* sales had increased in each country that implemented the program. Think of that: A tool that could more than double the exposure of key messages to your target audience *and* increase sales—all for less than $10,000.

Myth #4: You Can't Measure the ROI, so Why Bother?

ROI is an accounting term that means return on investment. To calculate the ROI of any project, you take the total amount of money saved or brought in and subtract from it the total budget amount invested, then divide it by the cost of investment. That's the net return, and it is typically a measure of money saved, costs avoided, or revenue brought in.

There are some programs for which establishing a reliable ROI figure is not an easy task, but it is generally doable. For example, suppose you institute a new communications effort designed to increase trust in the organization, and you spend $50,000 on social media, public relations efforts, and community outreach. Now suppose that, as a result, the next time you go before the city council for a zoning board variance your request breezes through in one meeting. You've probably saved that $50,000 in legal fees alone. Or, suppose that you have to recall a product and your sales rebound in 3 months instead of 12. Again, the net gains far outweigh the cost of your outreach program.

Just because something isn't easy to measure, it's no reason not to measure it. Too often the people who are screaming loudest about not being able to demonstrate the ROI of their programs are those who simply don't want to try anything new. They are just using ROI as an excuse to say no.

Myth #5: Measurement Is Strictly Quantitative

Another myth claims that measurement primarily concerns quantifiable entities such as sales, leads, conversions, mentions, friends, or followers. The reality, however, is that the only type of measurement system that works combines both *qualitative* and *quantitative* data. If all you look at are sales and not the relationships your organization has with its publics, you'll never be able to accurately understand why those sales go up or down. To really understand your successes (and failures) you need to measure what I call "revenuetionships"—both the revenue you bring as well as the relationships and reputation that you build with your publics.

Myth #6: Measurement Is Something You Do When a Program Is Over

Measurement is seen too frequently as an afterthought, a tool to gauge the efficiency of a program you have already completed. On the contrary, in order to be maximally effective measurement should be in place at the start of a program.

Myth #7: "I Know What's Happening: I Don't Need Research"

I hear it all the time. And so often from managers who are generally quite effective, but who could be so much *more* effective if they only understood the true value of measurement. Measurement provides the context and the rationale behind changes in your reputation, your relationships, and ultimately your P&L.

Everyone has a formal accounting system to track and measure profit and loss. So why the reluctance to establish similar formal systems to track and evaluate other business processes like marketing and communications efforts, relationships, and reputation? Without such systems in place, you will never know why your sales rise and fall, or what you need to do to make them rise faster.

MEASUREMENT, THE GREAT OPPORTUNITY: WHERE ARE MOST COMPANIES IN TERMS OF MEASUREMENT AND WHERE COULD THEY BE?

Despite billions spent on marketing and communications, the percentage of companies who are actually measuring their marketing efforts is shockingly low. Study after study shows that most CEOs don't feel that they have adequate measures in place. And, despite or because of the rapid growth of data mining, the general consensus is that there's lots of data but very little insight.

Part of the reason is that most organizations don't allocate sufficient resources to measurement. The annual Annenberg GAP study of common practices in public relations for 2010 reports that the average corporation spends just 4.5 percent of its marketing budget on evaluation (http://annenberg.usc.edu/News%20and%20Events/News/043010SCPRC.aspx). Another recent study found that 79 percent of organizations aren't measuring the ROI of their social media efforts at all (www.mzinga.com/company/newsdetail.asp?lang=en&newsID=252&strSection=company&strPage=news).

In general, those organizations that measure do better than those that don't. Years of studies have shown that one of the key ingredients of excellence is the ability to measure what matters (www.cmocouncil.org/news/pr/2008/011408.asp. Also: http://

customerexperiencematrix.blogspot.com/2010/05/cmo-survey-measurement–isnt–our–top.html. And: www.lenskold.com/content/articles/lenskold_apr07.html). All the best performers on most of the Top 100 lists are what we call "measurement mavens"—they invest in metrics and research on a regular basis and use the results to continually improve their operations. Most of the companies on *Fortune*'s Most Admired list have had some form of formal marketing measurement in place for years.

What this translates into for most businesses is a great opportunity. As long as the competition isn't measuring, you have a huge competitive advantage. You can listen to your customers—and theirs—and act on the issues and opportunities of your marketplace. All while your competition continues to operate in the dark. You'll respond faster, your relationships with your employees and customers will be better, and your reputation will be stronger. The results will show in your bottom line.

CHAPTER 2

How to Get Started

"All truths are easy to understand once they are discovered; the point is to discover them."

—Galileo Galilei

If you are new to measurement, it's best to start with baby steps. An annual measurement program can be a sizable undertaking, and if your organization hasn't done one before, it is a daunting process. I highly recommend beginning with a pilot program, either a three-month benchmark study or a targeted program aimed at a particular launch or event. This relatively painless route will get people addicted to the numbers, and they'll invariably ask for more.

A note about measurement and politics: Your measurement program will eventually step on someone's toes. It is inevitable that your data will challenge some traditional wisdom, or put someone's pet project on hold, or at the very least change internal priorities. Somebody is not going to like it, and they will push back. The good news is that you will be basing your conclusions and recommendations on real data. The facts will be on your side. As long as you have confidence in your data, you're standing on solid ground. Once you've established yourself as a data-driven manager who relies on accurate data, your credibility will soar. And let's emphasize that: Accurate data is the key to both the success of your measurement and to the decisions you base on it.

10 Questions Every Communications Professional Must Be Able to Answer

Before we get into the specifics of measurement, you will need to have at hand some basic information about your organization. Work through the following 10 questions and do your best to find the answers if you don't know them already. What's most important about this exercise is achieving consensus among the people who will be using and/or contributing to the measurement data you will be collecting. Getting everyone on the same page is an absolute necessity before you can begin to implement a measurement program.

Question #1: What Are Your Objectives?

While it may seem facile and simplistic to actually put this question on the list, I am amazed at the number of people I've met with who cannot answer it. Or, even more frequently, they have objectives that are not measurable. You must start with a thorough understanding of your company's or organization's business objectives. And if they are not written down somewhere, ask your boss—you might have a very interesting conversation.

I sometimes help my clients through the process by asking them to shut their eyes and imagine that it is the end of the year, and they are celebrating enormous success: Corks are popping, champagne is flowing, and bonus checks are being passed out to everyone. What is it that they are celebrating? Another way to define your mission is to frame it from the opposite perspective. Suppose your department was wiped out tomorrow—how would the business suffer? Later in this chapter you will find a detailed step-by-step procedure for working with a team to develop measurable objectives.

Question # 2: Who Are Your Program's Target Audience(s)?

This is another question that may be pretty obvious for some companies, but it never hurts to get it in writing. The important thing is to define the audience as specifically as you can. No matter what your business or organization, the answer to this question is not "Anyone with a pulse." There is always, within any market, a set of customers who are the most profitable, the most valuable. These are the ones you want to target.

Question # 3: What Is Important to Your Audiences?

Once you've defined your audiences, you can go about determining what issues matter most to them: What inspires them? What scares them? What are they most passionate about? Where do they go for information? The closer you get to identifying an audience's passions, the closer you are to understanding why they are loyal to your company or brand.

Question # 4: What Motivates Them to Buy Your Products?

This is perhaps the most salient question for your measurement program; the answer will determine what you measure. You need to connect your actions with the ultimate purchase decision. If you sell a commodity product and what motivates purchase is price/value, then you need to measure the extent to which this concept is being communicated to your marketplace. However, if you are selling a service and what motivates purchase is the long-term relationship with the brand and/or the salesperson, then you need to be measuring relationships or brand engagement.

Question #5: What Are Your Key Messages?

If you haven't articulated them yet or don't know what they are, do research to figure out what messages will resonate most forcefully with your target audience(s). Key messages should reflect what makes people buy your product or services, or what distinguishes you from your competition.

Question #6: Who Influences Your Audience(s)?

Who else influences your target audience and what are the secondary influences on your business? Enumerate all the traditional media, websites, online publications, politicians, nongovernmental organizations, peers, educators, discussion groups, industry gurus, and so forth that your customers take into account when they decide to do business with your company.

Question #7: How Do You Distribute Your Product or Service?

Through what channels do your customers purchase your products? Which do they prefer? Which does your company find most convenient or profitable?

Question #8: What Are You Going to Do with the Information You Get from Your Research?

Never ask a question to which you don't want to hear the answer. Make sure you can act on all the information you get and can make changes and improve performance as a result. If your report is going to the CEO, you will have 20 seconds or less to get your message across, so your report must make an impact like that of a billboard. If it is going to marketing, the report should be short, but detailed enough to include brand data as well as corporate data. If it is for market research, you'll need to provide cross tabs, verbatims, and other supporting data. If it's for the VP of communications, you'll want to make sure your results provide a big-picture corporate overview as well as the details as to why certain results are what they are.

Question #9: What Other Departments or Areas Will Be Affected?

Who will be involved in implementing changes as a result of your measurement program? This is one of the most important questions, because without buy-in from all departments to change their behavior or strategies, your measurement program will be a waste of effort. Whoever might have to change as a result of your measurement needs to be involved in the process of designing the measurement program. Without their buy-in, change will not happen.

Question #10: What Other Measurement Programs Are Currently Underway?

What data do you have access to? What metrics are already being collected? You may be able to tailor new measures to complement existing ones. For instance, sales or lead tracking data could be compared to marketing activities and measures.

HOW TO DECIDE WHAT TO MEASURE: SUCCESS—ARE WE THERE YET?

Before you can achieve success, you have to decide how you'll know when you get there. Any businessperson will tell you that every program or strategy must start with measurable objectives. However, defining those measurable objectives is one of the hardest aspects of setting up any measurement program. People will argue for and against such metrics as ROI (return on investment or return on influence), ROE (return on engagement or return on effort), and all possible metrics in between.

Too often we get wrapped up in what we think the objectives are or in adapting the objectives to what's easiest to measure. It sounds obvious, but measurable objectives must be measurable. So if you are going to measure customer engagement you need a clear definition of what you mean by customer engagement, as well as a metric to associate with it. Does customer engagement mean they "like" you on Facebook? Or does it mean that they give you their e-mail address and permission to contact them?

For example, I was meeting with a manufacturing company recently and the first stated objective was "drive customer engagement." When I asked them to what end, they responded that they wanted "better relationships with prospects." Certainly a laudable goal, but again I asked, "Why?" The response was that the people they had engaged with in social media bought product sooner and thus shortened the sales cycle. *Voila!* A bottom-line impact—and the key to measuring exactly what matters to the company's business.

Here's a step-by-step procedure for choosing and reaching consensus on measurable objectives:

Step 1: Understand your background.

  List the desired outcomes of whatever you want to measure.

  List your key messages and rank them by importance.

  List your strategic initiatives and rank them by importance.

  List your key target stakeholders.

  List your key competitors.

  List your "influentials," the industry analysts, influential bloggers, media, or financial analysts that have the greatest impact on your sales process.

Step 2: Assemble everyone on your team, including staff, boss, and boss's boss. Ban all jargon from the meeting.

Step 3: Ask them what they mean when they say, "Damn, we just got our butts kicked!" Write down their responses on a flip chart. (If there are too many people on the team, this entire process can be done with an electronic survey.)

Step 4: Ask them what they mean when they say, "Congratulations, you really kicked butt last week!" Write down their responses on a flip chart.

Step 5: Ask everyone what their objectives are.

  Write the first one on the flip chart. Then ask, "Why does that matter?" When they answer, write the response on the flip chart. Then ask again, "Why does that matter?" Write that response on the flip chart. Then ask "Why?" *again*. Keep asking why until you have a true, measurable objective that relates to the bottom line. Be sure to choose a metric to go with each objective.

Step 6: Once you have all the objectives and associated metrics up on your flip chart, have people vote on which are the highest priority.

I use the little sticky dots popular at yard sales. You give everyone a page of them, at least 10. Tell your people to imagine that each dot is worth $1 million and they get to spend it against any of the objectives. It's up to the individual if they want to put them all beside one objective or split them evenly, but the point is to use up all the dots. After everyone has voted with all their dots, the objective with the most dots gets measured first.

Not only does this process get you a clear, agreed upon definition of "kicking butt," but it also sets you well on the way toward a perfect measurement system. By getting everyone to agree on a standard definition of success, you can far more easily judge your performance in the marketplace and relative to your competition.

MAKING THE BUDGET ARGUMENT

The silliest excuse for not measuring is "I can't afford it." The reality is that you are spending money already on various programs, marketing plans, and strategies. Doesn't it make sense to spend 5 percent of the budget to figure out whether the other 95 percent is working? To put it another way, if measuring results can yield $300,000 in savings, isn't it worth $15,000 to get the data?

Cost isn't as big an obstacle as it used to be because so much of the research is now easier to do and much less expensive. The rapid advance of technology continues to drive down the cost of doing measurement, especially data collection and analysis. We used to have to spend $3 a clip to collect articles, now they're available for free via Google Alerts. Web analytics software that used to cost $50K and more is now free from Google Analytics.

Even the expensive analysis tools are now being offered for free to colleges and universities. Meaning that if you tap into students at your local university, you'll get both their brains and their access to software.

An unfortunate result of easy-to-use low-cost research tools is that it is easier than ever to implement a poorly planned study and end up with a pile of useless data. So it is more important than ever to plan carefully for just what information you want, and what you are going to use it for. That's why this book puts so much emphasis on setting objectives and careful planning.

If you encounter resistance from management for funding your measurement program, ask them these two questions: How much money do we spend talking to our clients? Can't we talk better if we spend some time listening?

How to Ensure Accurate Data

Without accurate data you are wasting your measurement time and effort, and you may very well be making bad business decisions as a result. Also, you are undermining your future measurement prospects, your credibility, and your career.

The best way to ensure accurate data is to remove the causes of bad data. There are four reasons behind most bad data.

Bad Data Reason #1: Incomplete Assessment of Variables

The biggest blinders of all are the assumptions we all make about what causes something to happen. So you put a whole lot of effort and energy into a program and you expect web traffic, or registrations, or whatever to increase. And many times it does. But not always. And most of the time you don't know why, because you've left out some key variable in your analysis.

My company recently learned this lesson the hard way while working for a major military-related charity. We lived to tell about it though, thanks to good research and a little luck. After the charity completed an apparently fabulous PR job, we did a nationwide survey and found zero increase in awareness. Zip. At first glance, the entire PR program was a colossal failure. On second thought, however, we realized the target audience wasn't really everyone in America; it was actually just those people with a connection to the military. And when we narrowed our analysis to that target audience, awareness and relationship scores went up, as did likelihood to contribute and volunteer. We'd had the foresight to include a question about military affiliation in the national survey. But if we hadn't, we'd never have known that the program was a success.

It is very easy to start with the mistaken assumption that a company is in control of its environment. But it is often the presence of coverage or conversations about the *competition* that drives behavior concerning the organization you are interested in. Again, if you're not tracking the competition, you've left out a key variable that you will need if you want your research to be accurate.

Bad Data Reason #2: Relevancy of Content

Back in the old days there would be teams of people who physically scanned publications, selecting only those articles that matched the required criteria. In other words, it was a human brain that decided that the content was actually about the company or the product and had some bearing on a customer's purchasing decisions. Today's electronic searches are a big help, but they aren't very smart in certain ways. So we still need human reviewers to check up on things.

In some cases up to 90 percent of what you receive from an electronic search can be irrelevant. You need a very sophisticated Boolean search string to even get close to accurate results, and those still need to be checked by humans. Otherwise, you can end up with "I met a really sassy intelligent chick in the business school," when you actually searched for "SAS business intelligence software."

Bad Data Reason #3: Commercial Services Omit Results

Then there's the issue of omission. The average content provider picks up just a fraction of actual tweets and an even smaller selection of Facebook threads. If your provider says it can do better, do your own search on search.twitter.com or just compare with your average Google search. In roughly five out of six systems we tested, Google and Twitter outperformed the commercial services.

Bad Data Reason #4: The (In)accuracy of Content Analysis

After you've screened out all the drivel and have a solid database of mentions, you then need a way to accurately analyze that content. The fast and easy solution today is computer-automated sentiment analysis. There's a good reason it is so popular: Wouldn't it be wonderful to simply hit a few buttons to determine what customers actually thought about your brand? Well, dream on. Most automated sentiment analysis doesn't even come close.

First of all, most sentiment analysis systems get it right about 50 percent of the time, and you get what you pay for. A cheap system will get it wrong even more often. You need a sophisticated system supplemented with human coders to get anywhere close to accurate results.

Secondly, no amount of automated sentiment analysis can tell you what people are actually thinking. To know this you need to ask them.

What automated sentiment analysis actually does is report the most common words that people are using to discuss or write about your product or services. Lots of times computers can misinterpret those words. Most computers don't understand the irony and sarcasm typical of today's conversations. If I say, for instance, that I found a "wicked cool restaurant," the computer has no way of knowing that I'm from New England and that's a compliment. Worse still, if I mentioned that I saw the play *Wicked* after eating at that wicked cool dining spot, a computer might think I'm suggesting burning the restaurant and all its occupants at the stake.

So what's an acceptable level of accuracy for automated analysis? If you can get computers to agree with human coders 80 percent of the time, you're doing really well.

A SIMPLE CHECKLIST TO ENSURE ACCURATE RESULTS

1. _____ Get consensus on the big picture issues:
   a. _____ Ask yourself: Do you really want the truth, or are you just trying to justify your existence? Are you, and your boss, really interested in reality, or is this just an exercise in budget justification?
   b. _____ List the audiences that will see and use the data.
   c. _____ List the objectives for the research.
   d. _____ Make sure those objectives are in line with corporate and divisional objectives.
2. _____ Inventory existing research:
   a. _____ Find out who is already doing what for research in your organization. If it is survey research, is it reusable? Is there leverage in keeping questions consistent?
   b. _____ Find out if your market research department has a reliable track record with a particular vendor(s). Do they have accuracy standards that you can adopt?
3. _____ Do your background homework:
   a. _____ Review Dr. Walter K. Lindenmann's "Guidelines and Standards for Measuring the Effectiveness of PR Programs and Activities" available at the Institute for Public Relations website (www.instituteforpr.org/files/uploads/2002_MeasuringPrograms_1.pdf).

    b. ____ Review the CASRO Code of Standards and Ethics for Survey Research (www.casro.org/codeofstandards.cfm).

    c. ____ Review the Measurement Guidelines from IAB (www.iab.net/iab_products_and_industry_services/508676/guidelines).

4. ____ Determine the universe within which you are doing research:

    a. ____ Will you investigate a defined media set or "everything?" (You won't ever really get everything; realistically, you'll get about 85 percent.)

    b. ____ Determine if you have a defined universe that matches your target audiences. Will it require sampling?

    c. ____ Test to make sure you are getting a representative sample.

    d. ____ List the variables that will be included. Get agreement from your boss and your boss's boss on those variables.

5. ____ Determine who will do the work:

    a. ____ If in-house, then:

        i. ____ Write up your methodology.

        ii. ____ Test your methodology.

        iii. ____ Refine your methodology until you achieve a minimum of an 88 percent intercoder reliability score.

        iv. ____ Decide if sampling error limits will be shown (if they can be computed).

        v. ____ Determine how projectable the research findings will be to the total universe or population under study.

        vi. ____ Analyze your results, using correlations wherever possible.

    b. ____ If you're outsourcing research:

        i. ____ Determine who will actually be supervising and/or carrying out the project.

        ii. ____ Investigate their backgrounds and experience levels.

    iii. ____ Determine who will actually be doing the field work. If the assignment includes media content analysis, who will be reading the clips or viewing or listening to the broadcast video/audio tapes? If the assignments involve focus groups, who will be moderating the sessions? If the study involves conducting interviews, who will be doing those and how will they be trained, briefed, and monitored?

    iv. ____ Determine and confirm that quality control mechanisms have been built into the study to assure that all readers, moderators, and interviewers adhere to the research design and study parameters.

    v. ____ Review the written set of instructions and guidelines for the readers, the moderators, and the interviewers.

    vi. ____ If the data are weighted, insist upon examining the basis for those weights (no black boxes allowed).

    vii. ____ Determine if sampling error limits will be shown (if they can be computed).

    viii. ____ Determine how projectable the research findings will be to the total universe or population under study.

6. ____ Review the results:

    a. ____ Do a "Does this make sense test?" For instance, if you thought you were fourth in the marketplace and the results place you at number one, ask why. If a competitor has a major product launch but its share of conversation declines, then what's up with that?

    b. ____ Ask "So what?" three times for every chart. Data is only meaningful if it tells you what to do next. Figure out the "so whats?" and the "what are the next steps?"

    c. ____ Dig into the negatives first: What doesn't make you look good is much more educational than good news that you expect.

CHAPTER 3

SEVEN STEPS TO THE PERFECT MEASUREMENT PROGRAM: HOW TO PROVE YOUR RESULTS AND USE YOUR RESULTS TO IMPROVE

"The only statistics you can trust are those you falsified yourself."
—Winston Churchill

The measurement of most business strategies is an iterative process: The strategy is implemented, data about its success is acquired and analyzed, and changes are made to the strategy. Then the revised strategy is implemented, more data is acquired, and more changes are made. And so on again and again. Most measurement programs, no matter who the stakeholders or what the metrics, proceed through this process with seven basic logical steps. In fact, in my 20 years in the measurement business, every measurement program I have developed has involved some version of these steps. These seven basic steps are discussed at length in this chapter, and they form the framework for most of the chapters to follow. The tremendous value of these steps is that you can adapt them to measure any program you might encounter.

A note about benchmark studies: It is very common to undertake some preliminary research to help you with the first few of these seven steps. For some companies and situations, your audience, benchmarks, key performance indicators (KPIs), and measurement tools will be fairly obvious. But for others you may have to hunt up some existing data or do a benchmark study or two before you really know what you are dealing with. For instance, you may have to start by surveying your audiences to find out what is important to them and how they get their information.

We almost always advise those organizations that have never done measurement before to do a simple preliminary study before undertaking a large project. Doing a smaller study will introduce everyone involved to the process of measurement and to the advantages of using the data it generates.

Note that the term "benchmark" is used here in two slightly different ways. A *benchmark study* is preliminary research done to learn about audiences or an environment or to set goals for future projects. A *benchmark to compare against*, which we discuss in Step 4 later in this chapter, is a standard against which you measure progress toward your goals. A benchmark may be set as the result of a benchmark study, or you might benchmark your results against those of your competitors.

STEP 1: DEFINE YOUR GOALS AND OBJECTIVES: WHY ARE YOU LAUNCHING THIS PLAN OR PURSUING THIS STRATEGY? WHAT IS THE "R" IN THE ROI THAT YOU ARE SEEKING TO MEASURE?

In order to be measurable, the goals or objectives of your strategy or campaign *must* include not just the desired outcome but also a date by which it should happen, and ideally, a budget and the audience it is designed to influence. Your answers should relate back to strategic corporate goals, such as increasing market share, owning a position in the marketplace, or, for nonprofits, fulfilling a mission. Chapter 2 includes a detailed step-by-step procedure for working with a team to develop measurable objectives.

Typically we find that most marketing goals fall into three overall categories:

1. *Sales*: The need to sell more product, increase market share, increase share of wallet, or increase online purchases.

2. *Message or Positioning*: This goal articulates a specific aspect of the organization's perception or reputation that needs to be changed or a relationship that needs to be altered. For example, the USO has had a problem in that its brand has been most closely associated with comedian Bob Hope, who for many years performed in popular USO events. Today, not only is that entertainer dead, but most of the people who recognize the name are as well, or soon will be. So the USO has needed to change their brand's image. Hence their Colbert-Goes-to-Baghdad program. Their secondary goal is to increase online donations, which in prior years represented only a tiny percentage of all charitable giving.

3. *Public Safety or Education*: This is most commonly a goal of government agencies and nonprofits such as the Red Cross, for programs that distribute information about impending disasters or disaster assistance.

A typical problem occurs when groups have mixed objectives. For example, one of the most frequently mentioned goals we hear is, "To reach our target audiences with our key quality message." This goal is great as long as the target audiences are similar. But what if one product group is targeting seniors and another is targeting college students? Quality may mean different things to different audiences. The best solution here is to create separate objectives for each specific population.

Step 2: Define Your Environment, Your Audiences, and Your Role in Influencing Them

Every organization continuously communicates in an environment with numerous audiences, including the media, prospects, customers, partners, employees, governments, communities, investors, thought leaders, and the international community. While you may think your advertising and public relations are reaching only your customers and your prospects, in reality it is probably seen by your other audiences, too. And with the help of the Internet, most of the time you communicate to those same audiences around the world.

You need to examine each individual audience and answer two questions: How does a good relationship benefit the organization? How might a bad relationship threaten it? Articulate what are the specific benefits of your efforts. The answers should relate back to strategic corporate goals, such as increasing market share, owning a position in the marketplace, or, for nonprofits, fulfilling a mission.

Equally as important, if you are measuring a communications or marketing program, is to tie the communications activity back to sales. For years there was a theoretical firewall between marketing and sales. Social media has torn down that wall and put everyone in the organization in closer contact with the customer. So it is more important than ever to think through the role each employee plays in getting and keeping customers.

Step 3: Define Your Investment: What Will It Cost? What Is the "I" in ROI?

With the advent of so many new free tools to influence your audiences, it's easy to overlook the investment in personnel time they require. Which is why this step requires taking a hard look at the resources you are investing in a specific program. What is the level of personnel time? What is the opportunity cost? Are you adding resources or shifting them, and what are the consequences? This early in the process you will not know all the costs you face, but you will often have budget constraints or allowances that determine how much you can spend. The rule of thumb is to spend five to seven percent of your marketing program's budget on measuring that program.

Step 4: Determine Your Benchmarks

A key point to remember about any evaluation program is that measurement is a comparative tool; to decide if you are successful you compare your results to something else. The most effective comparisons are to your competition and peers over time, to just yourself over time, or to an industry average.

Ideally you would benchmark against two or three competitors: A stretch goal, a peer company, and an underdog who's just beginning to nip at your heels (see Figure 3.1). Remember, even if you're in the nonprofit sector, you are still competing for share of wallet.

The next most effective benchmark is to compare your company to its past performance. If possible, don't just arbitrarily pick a calendar year or quarter; choose your benchmark(s) so you can track the results of a significant event, such as when a new CEO joined the company or when a new agency signed on. While this will tell you how your performance is improving or declining, it won't tell you anything about how you are doing relative to the market. So, if at all possible, track your competitors, too.

Step 5: Define Your Key Performance Indicators: What Are the Metrics You Will Report With?

Once you've agreed upon your objectives, defined your audience, and established who or what you will benchmark against, you are ready to establish the specific criteria of success, or key performance indicators, that you will measure. Each objective may require a different type of

Figure 3.1
Two typical benchmarks and how you would work with them. It's important that you define benchmarks appropriate to your company's goals.

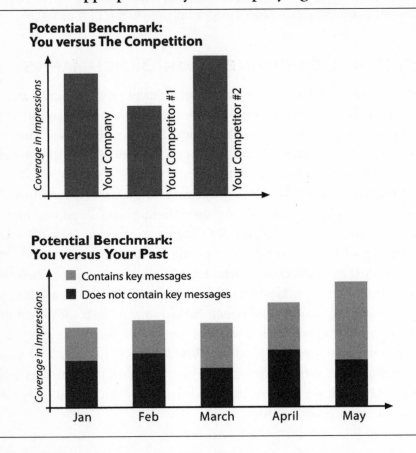

measurement and so require different KPIs. Some criteria are tied to output measures, like getting messages out to a particular audience. Others may be outtake measures, like raising awareness for your brand. And still others may be outcome measures, like getting people to attend your event or to download something from your website.

For instance, if your objective is to sell product, the criterion might be the incremental sales after a particular promotional program took place. If your objective is increasing awareness, the KPI might be the percentage increase of unaided awareness as measured by a survey.

Note: *Awareness* should not be confused with *visibility*. While years of advertising research indicate that visibility is linked to awareness, they are not the same thing. Visibility in terms of media coverage typically refers to either volume of coverage or to where in the story a brand or company name appeared, for example, in a headline or top 20 percent of the story. Awareness refers to a person's knowledge of a brand or message and is only measured by a survey, generally a combination of unaided and aided recall.

So if greater awareness is your objective, one strategy would be to raise visibility to get your brand name out more prominently than the competition. This doesn't just mean more articles. It means more mentions of the company name in headlines, captions, and other places of greater visibility.

Therefore, if visibility is your definition of success, the metric would be share of highly visible coverage, for instance the percent of articles featuring your company name in the headline versus the competition. That data could then be compared to ongoing brand awareness studies to compare the impact of your earned media with that of your paid media.

A common element of marketing programs is to establish company spokespeople as industry leaders or reliable sources on topics of interest. In this case a goal could be to boost your share of quotes to be equal to or greater than that of the competition by some particular point in time. Obviously, if your spokesperson is getting quoted more often than the owner of a competitive franchise, then your program is more effective.

STEP 6: SELECT THE RIGHT MEASUREMENT TOOL AND VENDORS AND COLLECT DATA

Your measurement tools are the techniques you will use to collect data. (Measurement tools are covered in detail in the next chapter.)

Remember that any tool is useless unless it collects the sort of data that will help you evaluate your progress toward your goals. In most cases, you will be collecting data in one of three ways:

1. Content analysis of social or traditional media.
2. Primary research via online, mail, or phone survey.
3. Web analytics.

Not only do your tools need to collect the right data, they must be affordable and provide the data when you need it. At one company I worked for we did all of our planning in August, yet the yearly evaluation of our marketing programs occurred in January. Thus the data we worked with while planning was six months out of date. And the new data wouldn't be available until the following January, giving rise to the oft-repeated groan, "If we only had the analysis now." *On time* for most companies means that you have a report in hand when it is of value, that is, as you start your planning.

STEP 7: TURN DATA INTO ACTION: ANALYZE DATA, DRAW ACTIONABLE CONCLUSIONS, AND MAKE RECOMMENDATIONS

At its core, measurement is a continuous improvement process. For any measurement system to work, you need to assess results, make changes, see if those changes had an impact, make more changes, and so on. A very important element in any measurement program is the analysis of the data to arrive at valid, actionable conclusions.

Once you've collected all of your results, avoid the temptation to focus only on the most exciting. I've seen many reports gloat that "Press coverage increased by 50 percent!" but fail to mention that reach into the highest priority audience segment dropped by 15 percent or that the key messages about a particular product were never communicated.

To make information meaningful and actionable, relate each conclusion back to your original objectives. Compare your message communication this quarter to last quarter as well as to the same period a year ago. It takes a year or more to really change perceptions, so be realistic about your expectations.

As a history major working in engineering companies, I quickly learned that the key to communication with my top management was to use language they could understand. The language of business is charts and graphs. Therefore, to put measurement to work for you, you must learn to translate your raw numbers into charts and graphs with short headlines that draw conclusions from the data. Once you've done so, you're one step closer to actionable information.

Ideally, whenever you need to decide what tactic to use, what resources to pull in, or what spokesperson or message to emphasize, you will have up-to-date data at your fingertips. For that reason you need to set up a regular reporting schedule, so that in addition to demonstrating results, you can also get buy-in to changes in the program.

Five Ways to Measure ROI

The ultimate question is, of course, "What's the ROI?" In some respects, ROI is deceptively simple: "R" means the return you expect, and "I" is the investment you have made, (staff time plus agency time plus executive time plus hard costs). Subtract the I from the R and you have ROI. And, while pulling together the costs is relatively straightforward, calculating the actual return is anything but. We see five ways to determine the return:

1. *Sales or Revenue.* This is obviously the most direct and simple definition of ROI. If you are like Southwest Airlines, you can use your web analytics and customer relationship management (CRM) to tie actual sales to social media activity. This works well if you are selling tickets or managing an online sales site. It also works well for nonprofits where the goal is to increase donations.

2. *Cost Savings.* More and more organizations are experimenting with social media for marketing, recruitment, or customer service. By carefully listening to the conversation they are able to identify better candidates or more quickly solve customer problems. For example, food service company Sodexo calculated a $300,000 savings in recruitment costs after it began using Twitter to aid recruitment (www.sodexousa.com/usen/newsroom/press/press09/sncrexcellenceaward.asp).

3. *Paid versus Earned Search Rankings.* Most companies are spending significant funds on services such as Google AdWords to ensure that when customers search the Internet for their products, the company shows up high in the search results. One of the benefits of a proactive social media campaign is that it makes your brand more current and more relevant, two criteria that determine how high up in a search your brand will appear. Many companies that have active social media campaigns find that they can drop their paid search ads altogether and still receive very high rankings in search.

4. *Cost Avoidance.* Any company or brand has the potential to be caught in a crisis. Whatever the nature of that crisis, good relationships can help mitigate its extent and duration. The best way to calculate the value of that mitigation is to examine what happens to competing organizations in your marketplace. For instance, compare the money spent on legal fees for a crisis that was mitigated with the help of an active social media presence to one handled without the benefit of social media.

5. *Social Capital.* There has been extensive research done by Robert Putnam and others on the value of social capital and social networks (http://bowlingalone.com/). His work shows that, for an individual, the more relationships you have the better your life is, the longer you live, and the healthier you are. For a company, good social capital means that information flows more easily, innovation and efficiency increase, and legal costs go down.

You can extend this concept to social media. If a blog is generating favorable comments, engaging employees or customers in the business of the organization, and disseminating information quickly and accurately, it is contributing to the social capital of your organization. To measure results in this case you will need tools to both monitor and analyze the conversations, as well as data from other parts of your organization on business processes such as customer turnover rates, employee turnover rates, legal costs, and productivity scores (typically measured in revenue per employee).

How to Leverage Your Measurement Results to Get What You Want

You will never be as powerful or persuasive as when you present your results to your bosses, so plan your presentation according to what actions you might want them to take:

- *Ask for money.* Many clients I've worked with have asked for and received additional budgetary dollars immediately after presenting their results, just on the strength of their measurement programs and insights.
- *Get commitment.* Have you ever had a hard time persuading executives to go on press tours? Show them a chart to indicate the potential disaster if they don't go.
- *Manage timing.* To demonstrate how effective strategic timing can be, present your results in graphs and charts that show changes over time.
- *Buy influence.* Use your results to win other departments over to your point of view and approve your programs.
- *Get outside help.* You may want to convince your bosses that you need more help to achieve the results they desire. The coverage of one of our clients skyrocketed in August and continued at vastly increased rates. I couldn't figure out what happened until I learned that the client had doubled its staff in July.

- *Just say no.* By using your results to demonstrate what doesn't work, you can frequently dissuade managers and colleagues from repeating mistakes. Has a product manager ever asked you to do a party or a press conference just because it would be "a fun way to introduce the product?" Say "no" by showing the manager a chart demonstrating, for example, that a press tour communicates your key messages much more effectively.

CHAPTER 4

Yes, You Can Afford to Measure: Choosing the Right Measurement Tool for the Job

"One accurate measurement is worth a thousand expert opinions."
—Rear Admiral Grace Murray Hopper

While the fundamental techniques of statistics and research design don't change much over the years, the ability of new technologies to get interesting data into our hands does change rapidly. Measurement tools and systems have advanced tremendously in the last decade or so. Gathering data, whether from media outlets or customers, becomes faster and cheaper every year, and new tools and techniques are developed all the time. Electronic access to data from thousands of media outlets combined with automated content analysis has revolutionized the clipping and content analysis business. You can now get daily analysis of your items delivered to your desktop 24/7. Rapidly advancing technology now allows the widespread use of web analytics and unique URLs to tie activities to actual user response.

The only way to stay on top of this change is to continually educate yourself. A good place to start is at one of the best research websites, that of the Society for New Communications Research at www.sncr.org. We also continuously update our readers at www. themeasurementstandard.com and kdpaine.blogs.com.

It used to be that the biggest barrier to measurement was cost. With the proliferation of inexpensive tool choices, the biggest barrier is figuring out just what tools you need. This chapter provides detailed information about the basic tool set required to measure any of your programs and how to best control your costs for those tools.

How to Decide What Tool Is Right for You: The Right Tool Depends on the Job

Even the most sophisticated measurement tool is worthless if it can't measure progress toward your goals. If your goal is awareness, for instance, no amount of simple media content analysis will tell you if you are achieving it. You must use some technique that will measure the degree to which your publics are truly aware of your brand, your brand benefits, or your messages. See Figure 4.1 for some examples of program objectives, typical metrics for measuring those objectives, tools to gather the data, and sample vendors to supply those tools. These are just a few examples from the great many options available; what you actually use will depend on the details of your program.

If you are new to measurement, start with a basic program that uses simple tools. Ultimately you will want to establish a system that measures your processes, your outputs (Did you communicate often enough? Did you generate enough content?), your outtakes (What did your publics take away from your efforts?), as well as your outcomes (Did the behavior of your stakeholders change?). These last three divisions we will address in this chapter as: What they are *saying* (outputs), what they are *thinking* (outtakes), and what they are *doing* (outcomes).

Figure 4.1

You must select measurement tools that can best measure your goals.

The Right Tools for the Job

Objective	Metric	The Right Tool and Sample Vendors
Inquiries Web traffic Recruitment	Percent increase in traffic Clickthroughs or downloads	Web server analytics, e.g., Clicktrax or WebTrends
Preference	Percent of audience preferring your brand to the competition	Online surveys, e.g., SurveyMonkey or Zoomerang
Awareness	Percent awareness of your product Cost per impression	Online surveys, e.g., SurveyMonkey or Zoomerang
Communicate messages	Percent of articles containing key messages Total opportunities to see key messages Cost per opportunity to see key messages	Media analysis, e.g., Clipmetrics, DIY Dashboard, Cymfony, Biz360, Vocus, MediaSense, Echo, or CARMA
	Percent aware of or believing in key messages	Surveys

TOOLS TO DETERMINE WHAT YOUR MARKETPLACE IS SAYING: MEDIA CONTENT ANALYSIS

In an ideal world, you would poll your entire audience to see what they read and how they react to everything you do. A more realistic alternative involves reading and quantifying what people are saying about you, whether it is in the traditional print and broadcast media or online in social networks, blogs, microblogs, and communities. This technique is called *media content analysis*, and it is one of the most valuable and commonly used tools in measurement. Several excellent books on the subject are listed in Appendix 2. Some aspects of media content analysis that are specific to social media are discussed in Chapter 5; see "Content Analysis: The Tool to Measure the Conversation." If your objective is exposure and communication of key messages, measuring media content is essential. In the past, people believed output measurement was simply counting numbers of all the mentions or column inches that appeared in the media. But with the proliferation of social media channels, measuring what they are saying about you encompasses far more than calculating sheer volume. It includes looking at the content of each item to determine whether it contains your key messages, how the article leaves the reader feeling, and what messages it communicates. In other words, you need to measure the *quality* of your output as well as the *quantity*.

To understand this, consider the following example. Which do you think demonstrates a more successful public relations program: a fat notebook containing 500 items or a skinny little folder containing 75 items? The answer, of course, is *neither*. Without examining the content, you have no way of knowing. The former might represent a surge in negative references about the company. The latter might represent a program in which the client communicated its key messages in a whopping 75 percent of the items, and reached all of its target audiences and 95 percent of its key publications.

As an example, look at United Airlines' "United Breaks Guitars" music video fiasco. Produced by a disgruntled passenger, this humorous and highly critical piece appeared on YouTube and generated millions of impressions and page views. None of it was of a desirable kind.

Media content analysis can be done with human readers, or it can be automated with computers (see Figure 4.2). While computer

Figure 4.2
Comparison of Manual and Automated
media content analysis.

Media Content Analysis: Manual or Automated?

Tool	Strengths	Limitations
Automated content analysis	Can analyze large volumes of articles very quickly to determine share of discussion, share of visibility, and share of positioning Very fast Very efficient	Doesn't pull out influencers and spokespeople well Doesn't determine tone Can't determine subtle or complex messages Many foreign publications are not available
Manual content analysis	Excellent for pulling out complex messaging, tonality, and subtle differences	Usually slow and cumbersome Readers can be biased or inconsistent

analysis can be effective at some very gross measures such as volume of discussion compared to the competition over time, it is highly unreliable for more subtle aspects such as detecting key messages. Computers are also lousy at differentiating between irony and sarcasm, and they are not likely to pick up regional variations. If I say that I had a "wicked good meal at the local Chinese restaurant," the computer doesn't know I'm from northern New England and that "wicked" translates to "very." Or, if I say, "Yeah, saw the movie, read the book," the computer can't figure out if I'm recommending the book or panning the movie. Our recommendation is to use computers to do the heavy lifting, and use humans to detect the subtleties.

The following is a list of the most common elements that are coded for in a content analysis.

Type of Media

Today there are literally dozens of places (typically called *channels*) in which your company can be discussed. Among them are:

- Blogs and comments
- Forums
- Micromedia (Twitter)
- Comments
- Photo sharing sites like Flickr
- Podcasts
- Video sharing sites like YouTube
- Social bookmarking
- Forums/message boards
- Social networks
- Communities
- Print media
- Broadcast media
- Online news media

For each of these the author, reporter, or creator of the conversation has a different level of influence, typically called *authority*. Authority used to be determined by the circulation of a publication, so a reporter with the *New York Times*, with a circulation of over 1 million readers, had more authority than a reporter with the *Berlin Daily Sun*, with a circulation of under 10,000. However, with the arrival of social media, many of the most influential online sites may only have a few readers, but if their posts get picked up by the *New York Times*, they carry a lot of weight. See Chapter 5 for specific details for defining the authority of writers in social media.

Visibility: Prominence + Dominance

There is a great deal of evidence that shows that the more visible your brand is in a mention, the more likely it is that the brand and message will be remembered. Prominence is defined as the location of the first mention of the company within an item. So typically you would track whether the brand was first found in:

- *Headline:* The company is first mentioned in the headline.
- *Top 20 percent:* The company is first mentioned in the top 20 percent of the item body.
- *Bottom 80 percent:* The company is first mentioned in the bottom 80 percent of the item body.

  Additionally, memorability is increased if your brand is mentioned throughout an item, rather than just mentioned in passing. We recommend classifying each mention as one of the following:
- *Exclusive:* Only the company or brand studied is included in the article.
- *Dominant:* The company is the main focus of the item but not the only company mentioned.
- *Average:* The mention of the company is one of many integral parts of the story or is equal to other parts.
- *Minimal:* No one would miss it if the mention of the company were gone.

Tone

The tone of an article or mention is the attitude or opinion it expresses toward something or someone. Tone is broken down into the following categories:

- *Positive:* After reading the article you are more likely to work with, purchase from, refer to a friend, or improve your opinion of this company. The coverage is desirable.
- *Neutral:* The item doesn't give you enough information to form an opinion of positive or negative.
- *Balanced:* The item gives information that is equally positive and negative.

- *Negative:* After reading the article you are less likely to work with, purchase from, refer to a friend, or improve your opinion of this company. The coverage is undesirable.

Messages Communicated

Whether online or in print, the conversation about your brand can convey a variety of messages; some are desirable, some are not. You will want to track key messages established by the company as well as the opposite of those messages. Typically the rating would be:

- Enhanced key message
- Full key message
- Partial/incomplete message
- No message
- Wrong or opposite message

Sources Mentioned

Influencing the influencers is key for almost all successful programs. So you will want to know if financial analysts, industry gurus, vital customers, user groups, and so forth are picking up your key messages. Who is quoted in your coverage and what do they say?

Conversation Type

The nature of the conversations in social media as well as traditional media can tell you a great deal about what people are saying and thinking about you. Our research shows that there are 27 types of conversations that take place:

1. Acknowledging receipt of information
2. Advertising something
3. Answering a question
4. Asking a question

5. Augmenting a previous post
6. Calling for action
7. Disclosing personal information
8. Distributing media
9. Expressing agreement
10. Expressing criticism
11. Expressing support
12. Expressing surprise
13. Giving a heads-up
14. Responding to criticism
15. Giving a shout-out
16. Making a joke
17. Making a suggestion
18. Making an observation
19. Offering a greeting
20. Offering an opinion
21. Putting out a "Wanted for Free" ad
22. Rallying support
23. Recruiting people
24. Showing dismay
25. Soliciting comments
26. Soliciting help
27. Starting a poll

TOOLS TO DETERMINE WHAT YOUR MARKETPLACE IS THINKING: OPINION RESEARCH AND SURVEYS

If your objective is to increase product or service awareness or preference, or your goal is to educate an audience, you need a tool that measures opinion—essentially the outcome of what you've done. Opinion research is by far the oldest and most widely used form of measurement. Pre- and post-surveys are commonly used to determine if a particular program changed opinions or awareness. An

Figure 4.3

Comparison of Survey Tools. Choose the survey tools that best fit your program.

Survey Tools Compared

Tool	Strengths	Limitations
Online Survey	Easy to program Fast Inexpensive Self-selecting audience	Most are English only Convenience sample (only those who have e-mail addresses)
Paper Survey	Slow More time to code and analyze Self-selecting audience	Better sampling (reaches everyone)
Phone Survey	High response rates Fast	More expensive

initial study establishes a baseline, and a follow-up study determines if opinion has shifted. See Figure 4.3.

Traditionally, most surveys and polling have been conducted by telephone. However, the Do Not Call rules have made this more difficult. In addition, more and more households are cancelling their landlines and using cell phones only, and there is no readily available phone book in which to find them.

So most organizations have turned to online surveys to collect opinions. They are cheap and relatively easy to field. However, they are only valid if all of your publics have equal access to a computer and an e-mail account. While online audiences are to a certain extent self-selecting, the data has been shown to be reliable and, in many cases, far more robust than phone sampling. Phone surveys can be faster, but their real downside is that they can cost many times more than comparable online or mail surveys. While to many, mail surveys may seem quaint and bit old-fashioned, they are often the most reliable option if not the fastest.

Later in this chapter we discuss controlling the costs of surveys. For a complete list of survey research options, refer to Dr. Don Stacks' *Primer of Public Relations Research* (see Appendix 2).

A serious drawback for surveys can be the time they take to conduct. Typically, results from a mail survey take four to eight weeks. If you are in an industry that changes rapidly, you may not have the luxury of time. While I was at Lotus we conducted an annual image study, which was, initially, how we measured our PR results. But we were part of an industry in which the PR picture changed monthly, and I just couldn't wait for a once-a-year study to plan my next move. At the same time, I couldn't afford to do our usual big annual survey any more often. So, I developed an affordable content analysis system to provide feedback on my program on a monthly or quarterly basis. If you try to do this, but don't get enough media to analyze, I recommend conducting shorter "pulse check" surveys that can be administered very rapidly on a regular basis, typically every quarter.

Measuring Awareness

Awareness can only be determined by surveying members of the audience at which the program is directed. Your product or service may well be the best in the industry, but if no one knows your brand, it will be very hard to sell it.

If you are introducing a new product or concept, one that has never been seen or discussed before, it is reasonable to assume that prior to your activity awareness was at zero. If you already have some presence in the marketplace, you will need to establish a baseline measurement against which to measure any future changes in awareness.

Best practices for measuring awareness are covered in the Advertising Research Foundation document "Guidelines for Market Research." See Appendix 2 for more references.

Measuring Preference

"Preference" implies that an individual is making a choice. Therefore, all preference measurements must include alternatives—products or companies that are competitive or that are perceived as being competitive. To determine the impact of marketing activities on audience preference, you need to expose the audience to the specific tactic or activity (article, white paper, speech, etc.) and determine whether the piece leaves the audience more or less likely to do business with the company. This exposure can be done in focus groups, panels, or by surveying a randomly selected sample of the population. This last method will generate the highest level of statistical accuracy but is the most expensive of the three.

Measuring Relationships

No one would argue that using a thermometer is not a better measure of the health of your child than simply feeling her forehead. Similarly, in business you need a precise measurement tool to assess the health of your relationships with your stakeholders.

The easiest and most reliable methodology for assessing the state of relationships between organizations and their publics is a set of survey questions developed by James Grunig, Larissa Grunig, and Linda Hon at the University of Maryland. The development of this Grunig Relationship Survey was motivated by the authors' search for a way to assess the long-term value of public relations to an organization. Convinced that "the fundamental goal of public relations is to build and then enhance ongoing or long-term relationships with an organization's key constituencies," they set out to develop a method to measure the health of relationships.

The results of this effort are presented in "Guidelines for Measuring Relationships in Public Relations" by Linda Hon and James Grunig, a paper that can be downloaded at no charge from the Institute for Public Relations website (www.instituteforpr.org/

research_single/guidelines_measuring_relationships/). I encourage you to read at least the first several sections of this paper. Not only does it present in detail the ideas and research behind the Grunig Relationship Survey, but it also makes an eloquent statement about the nature and importance of relationships to the practice of public relations.

Hon and Grunig's research identified six distinct and individually measurable relationship components:

1. *Control Mutuality*: The degree to which parties agree on who has the rightful power to influence one another. Although some imbalance is natural, stable relationships require that organizations and publics each have some control over the other.
2. *Trust*: One party's level of confidence in and willingness to open oneself to the other party. There are three dimensions to trust: integrity—the belief that an organization is fair and just; dependability—the belief that an organization will do what it says it will do; and, competence—the belief that an organization has the ability to do what it says it will do.
3. *Satisfaction*: The extent to which each party feels favorably toward the other because positive expectations about the relationship are reinforced. A satisfying relationship is one in which the benefits outweigh the costs.
4. *Commitment*: The extent to which each party believes and feels that the relationship is worth spending energy to maintain and promote. Two dimensions of commitment are continuance commitment, which refers to a certain line of action, and affective commitment, which is an emotional orientation.
5. *Exchange Relationship*: In an exchange relationship, one party gives benefits to the other only because the other has provided benefits in the past or is expected to do so in the future.
6. *Communal Relationship*: In a communal relationship, both parties provide benefits to the other because they are concerned for the welfare of the other—even when they get nothing in

return. For most public relations activities, developing communal relationships with key constituencies is much more important to achieve than would be developing exchange relationships (Grunig and Hon, 1999).

The Grunig Relationship Survey is a series of agree-or-disagree statements that measure these individual components. This set of questions has been thoroughly tested and shown to be an extremely effective measure of how customers or members perceive their relationships with an organization. Typical agree-or-disagree statements from the Grunig Relationship Survey include:

- I am happy with this organization.
- Whenever this organization makes an important decision, I know it will be concerned about people like me.
- This organization can be relied on to keep its promises.
- I believe that this organization takes the opinions of people like me into account when making decisions.
- I feel very confident about this organization's skills.

The full list of questions to measure each of the six relationship components can be found in Appendix 1. For more detail on administering the survey, see this follow-up paper by Jim Grunig, "Qualitative Methods for Assessing Relationships between Organizations and Publics" (www.instituteforpr.org/files/uploads/2002_AssessingRelations.pdf).

The challenge in using the Grunig survey is that few organizations have the resources or budget to conduct such an extensive survey. A questionnaire comprehensive enough to measure all six relationship components is lengthy. It can take a long time to administer and for respondents to complete. In fact, that's the biggest complaint we hear about using it.

However (as Jim Grunig has pointed out in personal correspondence), you don't have to use all eight or so items for each concept.

The Hon and Grunig paper includes a shorter list of items that can be used to keep the questionnaire briefer without sacrificing reliability. You may decide that such an abbreviated version is more appropriate for your situation. If so, pay careful attention to which relationship components you wish to measure and which questions you need to ask to do so.

In your questionnaire you want to frame each question as: "On a scale of one to five, with one being do not agree at all and five being total agreement, do you agree or disagree with this statement?" If you are testing all six components of relationships, you need to use at least two and ideally three or four statements for each component. For the reverse questions, you need to reverse the numbers so that one is good and five is bad. Tally up the totals for each component and average them for your score on each. Then, for a final overall relationship score, add them all up.

Increasingly, organizations are selecting two or three of the Hon and Grunig statements and incorporating them into reputation and relationship surveys that they conduct by phone or mail or online. The most useful statements are those that tease out the weaknesses in a relationship. These are the "reverse" statements such as "This is an organization that tends to throw its weight around," or "This is an organization that you need to keep an eye on."

An example of this technique's advantages was a recent survey of subscribers to a utility in which respondents responded positively to generic questions about the organization's reputation. But when pressed to agree or disagree with statements on whether the organization could be trusted, the survey revealed that there was a high level of suspicion about the utility's recent actions. As a result, the PR department was able to address those concerns and rectify the situation by bringing in members of the media and key public figures to share more information and begin a better dialog.

The ideal way to conduct a relationship survey is to sit down with a representative sample of whichever stakeholder group you need to survey and ask them the questions in person. However, in almost all situations that's not feasible. The most reliable alternative is a survey by phone, but chances are that that is prohibitively expensive. Phone surveys run around $50 for a completed survey these days, which means that to get a representative sample of the complete U.S. starts at $25,000.

The most realistic approach could be a mail or e-mail survey. Online surveys suffer from the drawback of employing a self-selecting sample (only those interested in the topic are likely to complete the questionnaire), but the trade-offs in terms of cost and timing are hard to beat. They are particularly effective in measuring relationships with members of an organization that are all on a Listserv of some sort.

Measuring Engagement

The holy grail of online measurement is *engagement*, a term that has been defined in a variety of ways over the years. Engagement is generally defined as a visitor taking some action beyond viewing or reading, for example, commenting, registering, downloading, retweeting, and so on. When a visitor takes such an action, we assume that he or she is indicating an interest in the company or brand or product.

The reason that engagement is so important to today's marketers, and why everyone is trying to figure out how to measure it, is that engagement is the first step in building a relationship between your customers and your brand. And in this era of overwhelming inundation of data and messages, an organization's relationships are what will differentiate it from everyone else. Measuring engagement is a way to determine whether you are actually connecting with your customers, or whether you are just yelling ever more loudly.

The actual tools you will use to measure engagement will depend on the media you are studying. Most often you will use web analytics (see the following section) for social media like Twitter, YouTube, or Facebook. You will probably also want to use the Grunig Relationship Survey (see the previous section) to investigate the state of the relationships you have developed through engagement. We discuss levels of engagement and the appropriate metrics in detail in Chapter 5.

TOOLS TO DETERMINE WHAT YOUR MARKETPLACE IS DOING: WEB ANALYTICS AND BEHAVIORAL METRICS

The ultimate test of the effectiveness of your efforts is whether the behavior of the target audience has changed as a result. This is also the most difficult to measure because of all the various factors that can affect the results of programs a company undertakes. The most effective way to measure behavior change attributable solely to your efforts is to study specific programs carried out by your team. For example, a PR program designed to increase traffic to a restaurant or a museum, or a fundraising effort.

To test the impact of a particular new tactic, maintain advertising and other communications efforts at a constant level for a given time, typically 26 weeks. Collect data to determine the baseline level of awareness, web traffic, and sales. Then introduce your new marketing program and continue collecting data to measure changes in awareness, web traffic, and sales. If you are in an environment in which advertising or other communications programs are changing, and thus presumably producing changes in addition to the changes produced by your new tactic, then to sort out the various influences you will need to use factor analysis or other sophisticated statistical techniques.

With the proliferation of web analytics and business analytics, it has become much easier to determine the impact of various efforts. Any organization that uses e-commerce has a tremendous wealth of information on how, when, and where customers purchase. Customer service data can also indicate satisfaction (or lack of it) with various programs. Your website is a tremendous source of data that can be used to measure the impact of various programs. Most websites already use some form of traffic analysis such as Google Analytics, WebTrends, or Omniture. These systems can tell you very specifically how many people go to what pages on your site. So if you provide a specific URL for a specific press release, then you can track editors' and consumers' behavior as influenced by that press release by following the traffic to that URL. For example, by tracking visitors' behavior and purchase patterns from its unique URLs, Southwest Airlines has been able to attribute over $5 million in ticket sales to PR. For more information, read the paper at www.instituteforpr.org/ipr_info/you_are_now_free_to_link_pr_and_sales/.

WHAT'S IT REALLY GOING TO COST?

The rule of thumb is that you should allocate five to ten percent of your overall project budget for measurement; half for up-front research, the other half for evaluation. The primary driver of expense is the amount of data you collect. The more people you interview, postings you study, or articles you analyze, the higher the cost. There are many estimates of cost for both surveys and media analysis, but they change with each advance of technology. Your best estimating strategy is to prepare a detailed request for proposal (RFP) and submit it to a variety of vendors.

Controlling the Cost of Surveys

The following factors influence the cost of surveying an audience:

- *Number of questionnaires administered.* You can probably get most of the information you need from talking to 250 people. If you are skeptical, note that it's possible to get a representative sample of the entire United States with only 500 people. So don't get talked into surveying thousands if you don't really need to.
- *Length of questionnaire.* It's always a good idea to keep your questionnaire as short as possible, as that both holds down the cost and brings up your level of response. A quantitative survey should take no more than ten minutes to administer.
- *Cost of collecting names.* In some research (if you are studying an event, for example) you collect names and phone numbers during the event and then interview by phone after the event. That way,

you know what they remember about you, not just what their initial impression was.

- *Difficulty in getting people to respond.* You may need to offer incentives to get people to respond or repeatedly ask them to respond. Marketers, for instance, are notoriously difficult to survey; even journalists and doctors are easier. You also need to make sure that every member has an equal opportunity to participate. The more random your selection the better. Self-selecting groups—for instance, people who come to your website—are much less desirable, because people interested in your topic are more likely to participate, thus skewing your results. What you may *really* be interested in are the opinions of people who are *not* going to your website.

- *Customized versus syndicated research.* On any given day there are thousands of research projects going on that research firms and publications hope to sell to every company in a particular industry. Contact the leading research firms and/or industry trade publications to find out if there's a project that applies to you. Another option is to add questions to omnibus studies that regularly survey the population at large. The typical price is $3,000 for one or two questions.

Controlling the Cost of Media Content Analysis

Commercial clipping organizations charge between $1 and $3 a clip to gather articles, and analysis firms can charge upward of $10 per article to analyze the content. You can expect these costs to come down as technology makes this work faster and easier.

Another cost influence is the number of media outlets you are analyzing. Eighty percent of your most meaningful and effective articles will come from twenty percent of your publications. Therefore, the easiest way to cut down on cost is to cut down on publications and limit your search to the twenty percent that really matter.

Are you collecting everything, or just those stories that have the greatest likelihood of being seen? Many articles, even in your top-gun publications, will not be relevant to your study. Such articles would include coverage of weddings, minor promotions, and company events. Discard these articles.

And if you're still faced with more articles than you know what to do with, limit your selection to those articles that mention your organization in the headline or lead paragraph. That's all the average reader pays attention to anyway. These articles are the ones that are going to have the biggest impact in the long run.

Random Sample Your Content

Another cost-saving approach, especially suited to social media measurement, is to random sample your content. Random sampling is a standard research technique in polling and survey research. It has gained widespread acceptance in content analysis in resource-constrained environments. Assuming you are looking at a file of thousands of blog postings or tweets, you can take a random sample (1 out of every 10 items, say), and conduct a thorough analysis of that sample.

We recommend sampling by media or by organization. In other words, if you are analyzing conversations about five different companies in your industry, take a random sample of postings about each company. Alternatively, you can take a random sample by channel: 1 in 10 tweets, 1 in 10 blog postings, or 1 in 10 videos.

If You Have No Budget at All

Become someone's homework. My company, KDPaine & Partners, was previously located in Durham, New Hampshire. We were blessed by the proximity of the University of New Hampshire, which has an excellent market research lab. Most MBA programs and undergraduate colleges offer some sort of survey research class. With a bit of luck and persuasion, you can get them to conduct the research for you.

QUALITATIVE VERSUS QUANTITATIVE RESEARCH

Focus Groups Provide Insight

Focus groups can help you probe to discover the real issues that concern people. If the major messages aren't getting through, what is? It is important to keep in mind that qualitative research (e.g., focus groups, one-on-one in-depth interviews, convenience polling) is usually open-ended, free response, and unstructured in format. It generally relies on nonrandom samples and its results are rarely projectable to larger audiences.

Surveys Provide Facts

Although it may contain some open-ended questions, quantitative research (e.g., a poll via telephone, mail, Internet, fax, or e-mail) is far more apt to involve the use of closed-ended, forced-choice questions that are highly structured in format. It generally relies on random samples and usually is projectable to larger audiences.

PART 2

How to Measure What People Are Saying about You Online and Off

CHAPTER 5

HOW TO MEASURE MARKETING, PUBLIC RELATIONS, AND ADVERTISING IN A SOCIAL MEDIA WORLD

"The difference between PR and social media is that PR is about positioning, and social media is about becoming, being, and improving."
—Chris Brogan

Thanks to advances in online technology that have made it incredibly easy and virtually free to publish, social media is turning the business world upside down. To paraphrase Ken Kesey, in today's media environment the inmates are now in charge of the asylum. A new blog is created every minute, and at one point during the June 2005 Iran election controversy, 200,000 tweets an hour were being posted to social micro-blogging site Twitter.

People—your customers, your employees, your stakeholders—are now the media, the editors, and the reviewers. They are in control and they're going to let you know what they think by voicing their opinions and changing their behavior.

From a measurement perspective, this social media revolution requires an entirely new way of thinking about what we do and how we define marketing success. We need to look at these changes as we would an earthquake. The tectonic plates of marketing and communications have shifted. As a result, some institutions will collapse and others will rise from the ruins. The degree to which you can get your mind around these shifts will be the degree to which your business will survive.

THE THREE-PART SOCIAL MEDIA REVOLUTION

Social media require us to shift our thought processes in three main areas:

1. Timeliness has been redefined.
2. The role of marketing and communications has been redefined.
3. Most definitions of success are irrelevant.

Thought Shift #1: Redefine "Now"

The most obvious change in how we approach business today has to do with the definition of timeliness. It used to be that if you got back to an irate customer in a day or two, you would be considered responsive. In social media time that is simply unacceptable. Back in the day, KDPaine & Partners had a competitive advantage because we could actually deliver reports to our clients within a week or two, instead of six weeks to two months like most other companies. Today, a two-week turnaround time looks downright quaint.

Here are some more examples:

- *Twitterville* author Shel Israel made the following comment on a minor squabble between prominent blogger Robert Scoble and social network Facebook: "It's been three hours and there's yet to be a response from Facebook."
- Domino's Pizza communications executives made the mistake of assuming that Friday was the end of their workweek. As a result,

a revolting video about conditions in one of their restaurants went viral. By the time they responded 48 hours later, millions had already watched the video and sales had already started to plummet.

- Frank Eliason changed forever the definition of customer service when he launched his Twitter account @comcastcares. Through Twitter, Comcast can respond instantly to customer complaints or questions. So, when I found myself without cable TV one Friday night in New Hampshire, I tweeted @comcastcares to see what the problem was. Within five minutes they'd checked my service, informed me that it was not an outage or other system problem, and suggested a fix. Exactly eight minutes after my initial tweet I was watching my favorite program.

There's no shortage of examples of how quickly reputations can be made or destroyed in today's social media environment. The lesson to be learned is in the redefinition of "timely." I suggest that timely today means you deal with a problem before it goes viral. Ideally, before more than a few friends of a social media user have seen it. And so to be timely in this social media environment, brand monitoring must be at least a daily process, if not hourly.

More important, if there is a crisis you must be prepared with a very rapid response. You need to have identified your brand influencers in advance, you must be aware of the issues and topics they will respond to, and you must have an internal action plan from which to operate. And, believe me, most traditional crisis communications plans won't work. Authenticity and transparency is paramount. Any obfuscation or dissembling will be found out and make matters worse.

Thought Shift #2: Redefine PR, Advertising, Marketing, and Corporate Communications

Internet technology now allows consumer decision-making to be based on reputation and online search, which, in turn, has changed

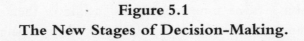

Figure 5.1
The New Stages of Decision-Making.

the role of marketing and communications. In today's environment, most consumer decisions are influenced in some way by social media and search engines. If someone is trying to decide what flat screen TV to buy, where to go for vacation, what movie to see, or where to make reservations for dinner, then chances are he or she will ask friends on Facebook or Twitter for advice and will search on Google, Yahoo!, or Bing for reviews. This new paradigm looks a lot like Figure 5.1.

Searches seldom begin with a brand name, but rather start with a category or a problem that needs to be solved. For instance, "best laptop for presentations," or "cheap flights to Europe." When you search for a brand or a product, you may pay attention to some paid Google AdWords results, but chances are you'll mostly click on and read reviews by someone whose opinion you respect—a friend, a colleague, or perhaps a brand name media site. In other words, organic search results beat out paid search every time. And chances are you'll make a decision based not on the number of times you've seen the brand, but based almost entirely on the reputation of the source of the opinion. "Is it someone like me with similar needs? Is it a media person or a Twitterer or a Facebook friend who I trust?"

Here is an example. My company was recently in the market for an e-mail marketing service provider. All our research was conducted online, and our ultimate decision was based on feedback from other e-mail marketing customers—people like us—who had voiced their opinions on blogs and Twitter. We did not speak to a sales person until after we'd made a decision.

This process is being repeated millions of times every day: If your brand or products have been talked about anywhere in social media, your potential customers are reading about it. What this means for PR and marketing is that communicating to smaller numbers of the right people is far more valuable than reaching millions of faceless eyeballs via advertising. Consequently, the value of advertising is declining, and the value of friendships, contacts, and engagement is on the rise.

Unfortunately, most marketers do not yet understand this new environment. They operate with the outdated idea that social media is just a new channel in which to advertise, and they think they can use it to scream more loudly at their stakeholders. In today's environment, the notion that the role of marketing or PR is to reach millions of eyeballs or to generate quantities of column inches in newspapers is about as useful as a buggy whip.

The rise of social media makes the cultivation of relationships with stakeholders more important than ever. In order to encourage those relationships, business needs to shift from broadcasting to customers to listening to the stakeholders, acting as their champion, advising internal decision-makers, and building engagement with the brand.

Thought Shift #3: Change How We Quantify Success

Which brings us to the final shift in our thinking: How we define success. For years, marketers equated success with the number of impressions or eyeballs they reached. This was, rightly or wrongly, based on consumer packaged goods research that showed that if you reached enough eyeballs you could convince people to buy your product. Somewhere along the line, business-to-business marketers accepted this assumption and counting impressions became a key way to measure marketing success. You either bought those eyeballs via paid advertising or earned the eyeballs by getting the media to cover your story or brand.

But in the social media environment the sheer volume of impressions is impossible to calculate and really doesn't matter. Social media encourages the development of relationships between people and products and/or organizations. And measuring these relationships, often by assessing engagement, is the key to quantifying success in social media.

THE NEW RULES FOR PR AND SOCIAL MEDIA

The nature of social media means that PR and marketing people need to completely rethink their approach. We must change from pitching to listening, and from measuring eyeballs to measuring engagement.

New Rule #1: You're Not in Control—and Never Have Been

The normal maxim for measurement is, "If you can't measure it, you can't manage it." The nature of social media renders management both impossible and undesirable. You simply can't manage what billions of independent, opinionated people are going to say. And woe to those who try; social media can resemble a cornered porcupine—very prickly—when it senses someone trying to control it. Just as you can't control a conversation at a cocktail party, your attempts to dominate a conversation in social media will be met with scorn and derision, and people will soon block such attempts.

New Rule #2: There Is No Market for Your Message

As David Weinberger told the 2007 New Communications Forum gathering in Las Vegas, "There is no market for your message." People now have access to so much content and have so many ways to gather news and information, that the likelihood of your corporate message penetrating the clutter is virtually nil. So it really doesn't matter how many people you've reached with your message. What matters is what people do if and when they hear that message. If you listen hard enough to learn what the social community is looking for and concerned about, you might be able to persuade them to hear and respond to at least part of your message.

That's not to say that conversations and relationships on the Internet can't be influenced, just that it takes a new approach. The old command-and-control, top-down message delivery is no longer an option. James Grunig's Excellence Model of two-way synchronous communications (Grunig, Grunig, and Dozier, 1992) is the rule of the day. Consumers can now choose to accept or reject your messages, depending on whether they find them useful, interesting, or relevant. And, they'll be more than happy to tell you what they like and what they don't like.

New Rule #3: It's about Reaching the Right Eyeballs, Not All the Eyeballs

There are two problems with measuring success in social media via eyeballs. First, the numbers simply don't exist. It has become virtually impossible to accurately count eyeballs in social media. More and more advertisers and media types are realizing that "hits" really does stand for "How Idiots Track Success." Unique page views is the web traffic metric that has been long accepted as standard, but it's now suspect, given the enormous variation in this metric from different sources. Many systems that purport to count traffic in fact only count traffic to parent domains—for example, TypePad or Blogspot or www.thenewyorktimes.com—and can't provide information on subdomains. Additionally, many of the most influential blogs do not routinely provide circulation figures or any other data on people who visit their sites.

And it really doesn't matter anyway. In terms of business, it's not about how many people visit a particular site but what they do with the information they find there. What you want them to do is read your information and then pass it on to their friends and colleagues, or comment on it, or sign up for something. And *those* are the things you want to measure. No longer is it sufficient—or necessary—to assume that you've made an impression on a visitor. Now you can actually measure what your visitor does with the information.

New Rule #4: It's Worse to Not Be Talked about at All

If your customers are making decisions based on what their colleagues, Tweeps, and Facebook friends are talking about, it may be more harmful to *not* be talked about than to be discussed in negative terms. Because in social media, if someone puts something negative out about you, chances are good that someone else will leap to your defense. It's actually more damaging to your business if the market is talking about your product category but no one is engaged enough with your brand to care about it.

Put another way, if you're not part of the conversation, your competition will be. If you haven't participated in the conversation, fewer people will be engaged with your brand. And, if you're not listening to your market, you'll miss not just the damaging conversations but the conversations that can give you insight into the minds of the marketplace.

So, for example, when I was trying to decide if I should upgrade my laptop, I did a Google search for "lightweight laptops" and got way too many responses. I went to TechCrunch and Engadget, and found a ton of conflicting, inconclusive opinions. So I queried my followers on Twitter and my Facebook friends. Three out of four said, "Get a Mac," 15 percent said, "Stick with your Dell," a few said, "I love my Vaio," and there was one vote each for HP and Lenovo. Not a word was said about Acer, Toshiba, Panasonic, or any other manufacturers, so it never even occurred to me to look at any of them.

Another major reason why it's worse to be not talked about at all is that most journalists today rely on blogs for story ideas, to check facts, track down rumors, and to investigate scandals. So if you're not being discussed, it's very hard to convince a journalist that you are newsworthy.

Finally, there is a growing body of research demonstrating that companies that are most active in the social media space outperform their more recalcitrant peers. At least for the top 100 global brands, financial performance correlates with social media engagement. (See http://blog.seattlepi.com/microsoft/library/engagementdb.pdf.)

BUILDING THE PERFECT ONLINE MEASUREMENT PROGRAM

So knowing all this, and knowing that if you can't measure it you can't manage it, the problem of how to measure your social media success may seem insurmountable. However, companies have been measuring consumer sentiment for decades, and, in fact, have been measuring consumer-generated media since it first appeared. Compared to mainstream media, the locale may have shifted, but the rules and tools really aren't all that different.

The biggest challenge to a researcher on the Internet is the sheer enormity of the task. The good news is that technology can help you find your way, and there are dozens of organizations out there that will be happy to assist you in gathering your data.

The bad news is that the data you gather will probably have major gaps in it and may be of questionable validity. Even the most comprehensive search firms can only gather a fraction of what you really want. Automated sentiment analysis is only about 60 to 70 percent accurate. Organizations like comScore, Neilsen, Compete, and Alexa all have vastly different data. Also be aware that media sites that require subscribers to log on will not be included in most web searches or in impression counts.

What's important in looking at your own marketing properties is not how many customers have the potential to view them (i.e., counting eyeballs) but understanding what they are doing when they are on your sites. What this means for your blog, for instance, is that you are not terribly interested in the number of visitors, but you are very interested in the actions your readers are taking. Are they engaged? Are they more likely to purchase? Are they requesting more information?

THE TWO WORLDS OF SOCIAL MEDIA

The first thing you have to understand is that the social media online world is divided into two types of properties: sites that you manage and control yourself and sites over which you have no control.

You manage your own website, blog, Facebook page, Twitter account, YouTube channel, and so forth. These are very easy to measure, because they provide you with traffic information and you can also place tracking code from services like Google Analytics or Omniture on them. But the vast majority of conversations are taking place on someone else's sites or in media over which you have no control and where you may not even be able to identify the writer or poster. We will address both.

Measuring What You *Can* Control: Web Metrics and Engagement

The most important element of measuring your own sites is consistency. Ideally, you would select a web analytics system like Google Analytics, WebTrends, or Omniture and apply it in a consistent manner across all your properties, including your website, e-commerce site, blog, and so on. For sites for which you do not have the ability to put your own web metrics code in place, like Facebook, you will need to rely on the data that those sites supply, and you must gather and use that data in a disciplined and consistent manner.

Like most other buzzwords, "engagement" has come a long way from its original meaning of "an agreement to marry." Essentially, it started with the notion that a website or a blog was "engaging" enough to get a reader to begin to develop a relationship with the brand. People began to speak of measuring engagement. Not just how "sticky" the site was but the extent to which it enhanced the relationship between the user and the brand.

Communications professionals and marketers now want to measure a site's ability to create an experience that earns a visitor's loyalty and, with luck, his business. As a result, engagement now means everything from the number of times that a visitor returns to a site, to the number of comments on a corporate blog, to the number of retweets of a Twitter stream.

Engagement is critical for three reasons:

1. *Engagement is the first step in building a relationship between your customers and your brand.* And in this era of drive-by flaming and inundation of data and messages, an organization's relationships are what will differentiate it from everyone else. Engagement is a way to determine whether you are having a dialog, or you are just yelling ever more loudly.

2. *Customer engagement helps promote and protect your brand.* Engagement produces brand advocates, the proverbial "people like me" (PLM), that these days have much more influence and credibility than corporations. These are the folks who broadcast their enthusiasm for your brand to their friends. Years ago, my company's work with Procter & Gamble and General Motors determined that these people were the single greatest influence on sales. And when it comes to defending yourself against negative comments in the blogosphere, you can never have enough staff on hand. Besides, your own spokespeople will never be as credible as those PLMs.

3. *Customer engagement can make your products better.* Listening to those customers who are most actively using your products provides a virtual customer panel that can identify weaknesses and areas for improvement in your products or services.

If I'm managing communications for a nonprofit and my ultimate goal is to increase donations, I know that somehow I need to form relationships with potential donors. The stronger my relationships with donors, the more likely they will be to donate to my organization. And engagement is one way to measure the strength of those relationships.

It is therefore critical to understand the extent to which people are engaged with your products, company, or organization. The good news is that measuring engagement in social media is relatively straightforward. Here's how it works.

In reality, engagement comes in a variety of levels and intensities, including:

- Level 1: *Lurking*
- Level 2: *Casual*
- Level 3: *Active*
- Level 4: *Committed*
- Level 5: *Loyalist*

So, for example, let's consider a typical nonprofit organization with a typical potential donor/stakeholder. Let's call her Veronica, and let's call the nonprofit KDP. KDP's relationship with Veronica starts when she visits a website, meets a volunteer on the sidewalk, gets a direct mail solicitation, sees an interesting tweet, or a friend suggests she become a fan on Facebook. All those points of contact are potential points of engagement.

However, reaching Veronica's eyeballs is just an opportunity, it's not yet engagement. If Veronica is a website visitor or someone who has seen one of your tweets or YouTube videos but takes no further action, we call her a *lurker*. Essentially, you really can't differentiate a human lurker from an Internet crawler or some other automated engine, so the engagement level is zero. See Figure 5.2.

Level 1 Engagement: Lurking   If, however, Veronica sees something she likes and decides to "like" it on Facebook or bookmarks the web page, then a relationship has begun to form. This is the first level

Figure 5.2
The Phases of Engagement.

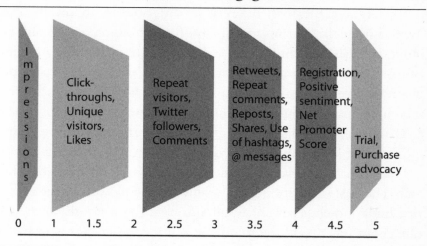

| Impressions | Click-throughs, Unique visitors, Likes | Repeat visitors, Twitter followers, Comments | Retweets, Repeat comments, Reposts, Shares, Use of hashtags, @ messages | Registration, Positive sentiment, Net Promoter Score | Trial, Purchase advocacy |

0   1   1.5   2   2.5   3   3.5   4   4.5   5

of engagement. At this point the relationship is pretty much pure exchange, to use the Grunig definition we introduced in Chapter 4. In an exchange relationship, one party gives benefits to the other only because the other has provided benefits in the past or is expected to do so in the future. In other words, it's just barely a relationship with no loyalty involved, but some sort of relationship has formed.

Level 2 Engagement: Casual   True engagement really only begins when Veronica takes some sort of action that indicates a desire to have further contact. It may be subscribing to a blog, following someone on Twitter, downloading a YouTube video, or suggesting a page to a friend on Facebook. I call these actions Level 2 engagement.

At some point, some percentage of these partially engaged fans or followers or friends will either get bored or become passive observers and the relationship stagnates. When it comes to measurement, the key metric at this point is one that will determine if the relationships are progressing. Therefore, you'll need to examine the ratio between new and repeat visitors and between those that come once and those that return more than three to five times a month. Twitter, YouTube, and Facebook all provide statistics that you can use to measure engagement at this level.

So, let's suppose that Veronica now decides to follow KDP on Twitter (implying permission to have further conversation) and, as a result, she sees content that she wants and enters herself in a contest. Both KDP and Veronica benefit, but there's no further expectation involved. Nonetheless, that action is a step up from no action at all; it's more than just lurking on a website. Therefore, to KDP or to Procter & Gamble or any organization participating in social media, it may indicate that someone has moved a step closer to a donation or sale.

Unfortunately, Level 2 engagement is where most relationships end. The vast majority of fans, friends, and followers never go past that initial point. That's okay, all you care about are the ones who care about what you have to sell. So our second engagement metric should be the ratio of eyeballs to people moving from the first to the second level of engagement.

Level 3 Engagement: Active   Now let's assume that Veronica hasn't gotten bored and is seriously interested in KDP's content. She has found friends with similar interest on the KDP Facebook page, is actively participating in Facebook or blog threads, is retweeting news updates from KDP, and sending out links to YouTube videos to all her friends. She's using KDP Twitter hashtags, perhaps messaging KDP directly, and is convincing her friends to do the same. She is now at Level 3 engagement.

Now the relationship is more of a communal one. As we saw in Chapter 4, in a communal relationship both parties provide benefits to the other because they are concerned for the welfare of the other, even when they get nothing in return. For most public relations activities, developing communal relationships with key constituencies is much more important to achieve than developing exchange relationships. Because when your relationships with your stakeholders are communal you will be forgiven for mistakes, you will get past a crisis faster, people will pay more for the product, and they'll recommend it to their friends.

So for Level 3, your key metric is the increase in Level 3 engagement over time, which you can determine by the analytics that most sites provide, for example, number of comments, number of retweets or @messages on Twitter, or number of repeat visitors.

What you really want to know is: What are you doing or writing or posting that has convinced all those Level 2 folks to go to the next step? What is convincing them to care more about you or your organization or your cause? You need to examine your activities, post by post and tweet by tweet, to see what is increasing the engagement level and bringing that stakeholder into a communal relationship.

Level 4 Engagement: Committed   If Veronica gets enough satisfaction from the relationship and her interactions thus far, she might be ready to move to Stage 4 engagement: registration on KDP's site or taking action on KDP's behalf. Somehow, from all that Veronica has learned so far about KDP, she trusts the relationship enough to provide her identity in the form of her e-mail address for registration or membership. What this means from a relationship standpoint is that the components of satisfaction and trust have been added to the relationship. According to Grunig, *satisfaction* is the extent to which each party feels favorably toward the other because positive expectations about the relationship are reinforced. A satisfying relationship is one in which the benefits outweigh the costs.

So your key metric for Level 4 engagement is the number of new registrations. What you should be measuring is the increase over time, not just the raw numbers.

Level 5 Engagement: Loyalist   But engagement doesn't end there; the ultimate goal is donations or volunteering. So to measure this, the fifth and final level of engagement, you need to look at Veronica's loyalty to the cause. How often does she contribute or volunteer? Is she bringing other volunteers with her, and is she expressing her commitment to the relationship to her friends?

While you can track Veronica's comments through Social Mention, Google News, or any number of monitoring tools, web analytics can't provide all the answers. Ultimately, KDP will want to survey all the Veronicas out there and find out how they're really feeling about the organization. This is where the Grunig Relationship Survey comes in. Ideally the survey would be administered prior to starting a social media campaign and then six months into it to see how you're doing on each score.

So is there one simple way to measure engagement? No, there are lots, and my engagement levels system is just one of them. But if you use this technique, you'll know a lot more than just "Are they engaged?" You'll know what is increasing engagement, what is turning people off, and how likely they are to act on your behalf.

Measuring What You Can't Control

Even if you spend millions and have a fabulous website, Facebook page, Foursquare presence, or what have you, the vast majority of the conversations taking place every day about your brand, your product, and your market will go on somewhere else, without any influence from you. Whether you like it or not, all of your social media efforts represent only a teensy tiny fraction of the conversations taking place in the marketplace.

While traditional marketing placed the emphasis (and budgets) on those things you can control—ads, direct mail, and direct selling—the new environment is so vast that even the largest budgets can't truly dominate the conversation, rendering the medium inherently uncontrollable. The best you can hope for is to learn from those conversations, make improvements, and maybe influence them. The following steps are based on the Seven Steps introduced in Chapter 3, and will take you through measurement of your social media presence on sites that you have no control over.

Step 1: Define the Goal   The first and most important question to answer is: Why are you starting that blog or Facebook page or online community? What problem(s) are you trying to solve? What do you hope to accomplish? And more important, what does senior management expect social media to do for the organization? If they don't know why you're doing it, you can't implement a measurement program. So you need to define—and management needs to buy into—the expectations and definitions of success. And if you can't identify a clear tie between your organization's goals and what you are doing in social media, then don't waste your time trying to measure it. As in any communications activity: If it doesn't support a specific corporate goal, why are you doing it?

Define Success

Before you do anything, answer the question: How will you define success? Almost all answers will fall into three broad categories:

1. *Sales or marketing gains.* If your answer is "gain market share," or "increase donations," or other such quantifiable revenue goals, then you will need a set of measurement rules and tools that emphasize web analytics. You will need to use unique URLs and some form of statistical analysis of traffic and response data.

2. *Increase engagement.* If your answer is "increase brand engagement," then you need to establish how you are defining engagement. For some that means click-throughs and downloads, for others it means comments and retweets. For still others, it's getting the visitor to leave an e-mail address, register for more information, or sign up for content. Procter & Gamble has challenged the media in which it advertises by indicating it will henceforth only pay for engaged visitors. So you can look forward to more specific definitions of engagement in the future.

3. *Improve relationships or reputation.* If your answer is "improve/ protect our reputation," or "increase brand loyalty," then your measurement tools need to include surveys, content analysis, and relationship metrics.

Step 2: Identify Your Publics and Determine How Your Social Media Efforts Affect Them   Clients often ask me if they should worry about Twitter, or if they should start a community blog or a Facebook page. I always reply: "Don't ask me, ask your customers." The most important factor in measuring success is to understand who your stakeholders and customers are and what interests them. So, first identify the specific audiences that you are trying to reach with your program. If there are too many to measure all of them, then make a list and prioritize them based on where your organization will see the most benefit.

Now make sure you can draw a connection between your efforts and the stakeholders whose behavior you are measuring. How does your social media program impact them? How does their behavior affect your organization? If, for instance, your company bans communications folks from talking to customers, it's going to be hard to make that connection. On the other hand, if you are on Twitter and talking to customers on a regular basis, then there will definitely be a link between your efforts and customer attitude or behavior.

Step 3: Define Your Benchmarks   If I tell you that 35 percent of the conversations about you are positive, is that a good thing or a bad thing? It could be that 65 percent of the audience doesn't care. Or that you just tripled your percentage of positive conversation from 11 percent the year before. If only 15 percent of the conversations about your competitors are positive, 35 percent is a great number. But if your peers are getting scores in the 60 percent range and you are at 35 percent, then you have a problem.

The point is that you need to figure out who or what you are benchmarking your results against. It could be a peer organization, a competitive organization, yourself compared to last year, or whatever keeps your C-suite up at night. If you select competing or peer organizations, try to limit the number of entities in any given study to no more than five. Three is ideal, and anything more than five becomes unwieldy.

Step 4: Determine the Specific KPIs by Which You Will Define Success Because you become what you measure, it is critical to carefully choose the metrics by which you will track your success. Presumably, the KPIs you select are the most important metrics for your organization.

Again, which metrics you choose should be driven by the goals you established in Step 1.

If Your Measure of Success Is Sales Tracking sales, donations, and/or memberships is the easiest form of social media measurement. Your metrics should include:

- Percentage increase in conversion rates
- Percentage increase in click-throughs to a specific URL
- Percentage increase in conversions
- Percentage increase in online donations
- Percentage increase in membership sign-ups

If Your Measure of Success Is Brand Engagement We discussed engagement in detail previously in this chapter in the section entitled "Measuring What You *Can* Control: Web Metrics and Engagement." See the metrics recommended in that section.

If Your Measure of Success Is Improved Relationships In many ways an increase in engagement is just another way to express the improvement in relationships and reputation that is the goal of any good communications program. Improved communications should lead to greater trust, improved satisfaction, and more commitment to the relationship. All of these can be measured through a survey of your audience, which will provide metrics such as:

- Percent more likely to express satisfaction
- Percent improvement in willingness to recommend (Net Promoter Score)

- Percent increase in trust, commitment, or satisfaction score
- Percent willing to buy or do business again (renewal rate)

If you incorporate some sort of relationship metrics into your survey, then it's much easier to diagnose the underlying cause of problems. Even though web metrics can track behavior with increasing accuracy, all the web stats in the world may not answer the fundamental question of "Why?" "Why did they stop visiting your site?" "Why are they spending less time there?" Or, more critically, "Why are they buying less?" So, an understanding of the nature of your relationship with your audiences will allow you to address the cause of behavioral problems you identify.

Step 5: Select a Tool   In the world of social media there's no shortage of tools. On average, someone announces a new social media measurement tool every other week. The reality is that many of these tools are irrelevant at best and, at worst, a waste of time and money. The tool you really need depends entirely on the goals you've set for your program. Which is why we always make selecting the tool the second to last step in the process of creating a measurement program.

There are three types of tools that have to be in your social media measurement toolkit.

Web Analytics and Statistical Analysis: The Tools to Measure Financial Outcomes   If your goal is sales and it can be measured by click-throughs and conversions, all you need is Google Analytics. Or, if you want greater functionality and sophistication, you can go with tools like Omniture or WebTrends. The key element in measuring contributions to sales is to accurately factor in the cost of that click-through or the cost of the lead. That means you have to factor in your time, agency time, and senior management time, as well as the actual cost of the program. This financial analysis allows you to determine the efficiency of different programs. Just remember to use unique URLs to most accurately measure results of specific programs.

For example, suppose it costs you $120 a year to set up a blog and you spend an hour a day on it. If you value your time at $150 an hour, your cost for the year is $54,870. If the blog generates 50 click-throughs a day or 18,250 a year, your cost per click is $54,870 divided by 365 × 50 or $3.00.

If the objective is not as directly commercial (if, for example, you want to move people along the purchase cycle), you can measure the number of people who click through from a blog to your site. The percentage of all visitors who take action or click through is a fundamental measure of success.

The most important part of web analytics is to make sure you are accurately correlating results to activities. Using a tool like SPSS or SAS, you will need to align the timing of activities such as product launches or announcements with the activity on your blog or website.

Surveys: The Tool to Measure Reputation and Relationships   As has been the case long before social media came along, if you want to measure awareness, preference, or perception, you have to actually ask people for their opinion. You do this via a pre/post survey, ideally beginning with a benchmark study before you implement your social media program, and then conducting a follow-up survey six months or a year after it's been in place.

Therefore, if your social media goal is improved relationships, you use the Grunig Relationship Survey; see Chapter 4 for a detailed discussion. To conduct the survey, there are free survey tools out there, such as SurveyMonkey or Zoomerang, as well as thousands of established market research firms. With respect to our blog example, it would be a great idea to conduct a periodic e-mail survey of just your readers (if you have a mechanism to capture e-mails of people who have visited your blog).

Content Analysis: The Tool to Measure the Conversation   Think of social media as one enormous focus group, with customers, prospects, employees, and potential employees all constantly sharing their thoughts with the world. Simply counting the volume of conversations and comments is not an adequate metric. While it might give you a good feeling to know that your brand is being mentioned with increasing frequency in social media, it would be highly dangerous to simply assume this to be good news. One only has to look as far as the recent social media disasters involving Edelman, Walmart, Dell, and Domino's Pizza to know that quantity of conversation may not be a measure of success. Therefore, you will very often want to determine the quality as well as the quantity of the discussion about your brand with a thorough content analysis.

We discuss media content analysis in detail in Chapter 4; see Tools to Determine What Your Marketplace Is Saying: Media Content Analysis. Here in this chapter we discuss some aspects of content analysis that are specific to social media, and we provide a detailed step-by-step guide.

Content analysis of social media gives you the opportunity to listen in on conversations. As a result, you will gain a much better understanding of how your audiences are responding to your initiatives. The words and thoughts shared in the actual social media conversations are an important source of information, and you should be looking for messages and themes to determine how your customers and constituencies perceive your organization or brand. How does the conversation position your brand on issues like employer of choice, value, or customer service? A good analysis will pull out recurring themes, complaints, and messages and quantify them to determine if they require action or can be ignored.

If you are dealing with a blog, you also need to determine whether the comments are in agreement or disagreement with the blogger, and what both sides are saying. Each comment needs to be analyzed in the context of the original posting to determine if the position is widely held or just an isolated opinion. Positive or neutral comments are indicative of a healthy relationship between the blogger and his audience.

Additionally, social media offers the opportunity to listen in on what your marketplace thinks of your brand. While it may not meet the strict criteria of market research, an extensive listening program (essentially a detailed content analysis) is in essence an online focus group that can provide continuous feedback on your brand and your product. Remember that you should be coding competitors' items for the same criteria you code for your own.

How to Conduct a Social Media Content Analysis, an Eight-Part Process

Part 1: Find the Content

Perhaps the most difficult part of any measurement program is collecting the content. All monitoring services have their own spiders and search engines, but none of them offer any guarantee as to what they collect. There are hundreds of millions of social media conversations going on. Not all conversations will be collected by every service, so you need to carefully evaluate the claims of the various monitoring services.

There are also a host of free monitoring services, including Google Alerts and Social Mention. Additionally, there are monitoring systems for specific forms of social media, such as Twazzup and TweetDeck, that are specific to Twitter.

Part 2: Determine the Type of Conversation Taking Place

Categorizing conversations by topic enables you to focus on certain conversations and ignore others. Looking at the type of conversations that people initiate or comment on can quickly tell you the nature of the conversations. By quantifying the percentage of conversations that fall into each category, you efficiently decide best practices in responding to or ignoring different conversations. Based on our own empirical research at KDPaine & Partners, there are in life and in social media just 27 basic types of conversation. See Chapter 4 for a list.

Part 3: Determine the Visibility of Your Brand

A key element in determining whether the discussion about your brand will be remembered and/or passed on is the visibility of your brand. Therefore, you need to determine where in the post or video or conversation your organization was mentioned.

Was it the focal point, or was it mentioned only in passing? Is the post entirely about your brand, or only partially about the brand? Here are some standard guidelines:

Dominance is the extent to which a company or brand is the focus of an item. Dominance is broken down into four categories:

1. *Exclusive:* The company is the only one mentioned in the item.
2. *Dominant:* The company is the main focus of the item but not the only company mentioned.
3. *Average:* The mention of the company is one of many integral parts of the story or is equal to other parts.
4. *Minimal:* No one would miss it if the mention of the company were gone.

Prominence is the location of the first mention of the brand or company within an item. The more prominent a name is in an item, the more likely a consumer is to remember it. So we can define the extent to which your brand is going to be remembered as part of the discussion by classifying the item in terms of its prominence.

Prominence is measured differently for text items and video items. For text items, prominence is categorized as follows:

- *Photo:* The company name is first found in a photo or in a photo caption.
- *Headline:* The company is first mentioned in the headline.
- *Top 20 percent:* The company is first mentioned in the top 20 percent of the item body.
- *Bottom 80 percent:* The company is first mentioned in the bottom 80 percent of the item body.

For video items, prominence is categorized as:

- *Video start:* The company is first mentioned or shown at the start of the video (first 25 percent).
- *Video middle:* The company is first mentioned in the middle of the video (26 percent to 75 percent).

- *Video end:* The company is first mentioned at the end of the video (76 percent to 100 percent).

Part 4: Determine Who, if Anyone, Was Quoted in the Item

If you are conducting a thought leadership program, tracking the presence or absence of your thought leaders is critical. Therefore, you need to determine where any of your leadership team or thought leaders are mentioned. If they are mentioned, did they convey a key message or positioning point? It is just as important to know what they are saying as what they are not saying.

Part 5: Determine Sentiment and/or Presence or Absence of Recommendations

Sentiment (also called tone) scoring in a content analysis can be seen as a substitute for a Net Promoter Score; in essence, you are determining whether consumers are recommending your brand. Net Promoter Score is a customer loyalty metric developed by—and a registered trademark of—Fred Reichheld, Bain & Company, and Satmetrix. The Net Promoter Score for a company is obtained by asking customers a single question on a 0 to 10 rating scale: "How likely is it that you would recommend this company to a friend or colleague?" Based on their responses, customers are categorized into one of three groups: Promoters (9–10 rating), Passives (7–8 rating), and Detractors (0–6 rating). The percentage of Detractors is then subtracted from the percentage of Promoters to obtain a Net Promoter Score.

The proper way to do sentiment analysis is an issue of some debate, because many companies claim they can use computers to automatically code for sentiment. In our studies we find automated analysis to be about 60 percent accurate. For instance, when a person from New England says that something is "wicked good" a computer will no doubt consider that negative. Similarly, if in a tweet about a movie I say: "Saw the movie, read the book," a computer will assume it is a recommendation for the book, not a panning of the movie. Therefore, we strongly recommend human coding for sentiment.

Typically, sentiment should be categorized as follows:

- *Favorable or positive* items leave the reader more likely to do business/join/support the organization.
- *Negative* items leave the reader less likely to do business with the organization.
- *Balanced* items have both negative and positive sentiment expressed.
- *Neutral* items convey no sentiment at all.

Part 6: Determine What, if Any, Messages Were Communicated

Assuming your organization has key messages it would like the marketplace to be aware of, you need to determine if they are, in fact, being picked up by consumers. Since it is highly unlikely that consumers will pick up your messages in their entirety, you need to categorize any discussion of your messages as follows:

- *Amplified message:* Writer communicates your key message and builds on it or amplifies it with photos, description, or recommendation.
- *Full message communicated:* All aspects of the message are included.
- *Partial message communicated:* Only part of your message is included.
- *No message communicated.*
- *Incorrect message communicated.*
- *Negative message communicated:* Writer says the opposite of your desired message.

Part 7: Determine Positioning on Key Issues or Battles

How was the organization (and its peers) positioned on key issues such as "good value for the money," "effective advocate for the industry," or "responsiveness?" Are you mentioned as an employer of choice, and/or as delivering good value? A good analysis will pull out recurring themes, complaints, and messages and quantify them to determine if they require action or can be ignored.

Part 8: Quantifying the Authority of the Writer or Poster

There are a number of ways to define the influence, usually referred to as the *authority*, of a social media writer. There are a number of online services, including Twitalyzer and Technorati, that assign grades to sites based on some variation of the following:

- The number of followers a user has.
- The number of unique references and citations of the user in Twitter.
- The frequency at which the user is uniquely retweeted.
- The frequency at which the user is uniquely retweeting other people.
- The relative frequency at which the user posts updates.

Authority can also be assigned based on the number of links to a blog site:

- *Low Authority:* 3–9 blog links in the last 6 months.
- *Middle Authority:* 10–99 blog links in the last 6 months.
- *High Authority:* 100–499 blog links in the last 6 months.

Another approach is to look at the specific industry and/or market and design an authority index around your particular business or market. This requires more in-depth bespoke research up front, but will yield more useful results in the long term.

Step 6: Collect Data, Analyze Results, Make Recommendations, and Measure Again   The most important part of any measurement program is teasing insight from the data and drawing actionable conclusions. So what if there's a big spike in positive conversation in June? The important question is: "What caused it?"

Ideally you would use a good statistical analysis package such as SPSS or SAS to determine correlations between conversations and web traffic or other outcomes. At the very least, you will want to determine what isn't working and what is. Look first for weaknesses, what didn't work. Then look for exceptional successes. Remember to analyze the competitive results as well. Where is the competition leading, where are you winning?

Then look at trends over time. What happened yesterday or last week is important, of course, but what you need to do is to see if complaints are going up or down over time, or if your relationships are getting better or worse over time, or if the ranks of complainers are growing faster than the ranks of supporters. Finally, keep close track of the activity to your website and correlate that activity against the various postings in the social media that mention your brand.

About negative comments: Do not—I repeat—do not go into crisis mode the first time you see negative comments. Do a bit of research first. Read the blogger's prior postings. See how many links and comments he or she has. If it's one or two, don't do anything, but watch the numbers; if they start to grow quickly, you may have an emerging crisis. If it's already in the hundreds, and/or if this blog is one of the most influential blogs in your industry, then you need to come up with a response. If the blogger is someone who has written hundreds of postings, but has received zero comments and does not appear on anyone's rankings, then you can probably ignore him.

If it's not a crisis, but there is someone who is consistently writing negatively about you, take the wait-and-see attitude. Evaluate the blogger's authority. See what kinds of comments are made, and how the blogger responds. Then start a dialog. Offer information, a different perspective, or new information.

A FINAL WORD ON ROI AND COMPARING SOCIAL MEDIA TO OTHER TACTICS

The ultimate question for social media mavens is, of course, "What's the ROI?" In some respects ROI is deceptively simple: "R" means the return you expect, and "I" is the investment you have made, for example, staff time plus agency time plus executive time plus hard costs. Subtract the I from the R and you have ROI.

Too often, however, what's behind a question about ROI is "I don't want to try something new," or "I don't understand social media" rather than a legitimate request for a specific metric. And, very often, these kinds of queries will eventually require that you compare the effectiveness or value of social media to other marketing disciplines.

Given the competition for corporate resources and the ever-increasing demand for results accountability, this is not an unreasonable request. But it is often difficult to comply with, and the temptation to use convenient but invalid methods is great. There are proven, valid approaches to comparing the value of marketing efforts, several of which we cover in this book. Advertising value equivalency (AVE) is a common and seductively simple technique, but is rejected by virtually every respected entity in our profession. However, since some people continue to confuse AVE with ROI, we are obliged to explain.

What's Wrong with Advertising Value Equivalency?

A number of people are calling for a social media equivalent of the popular but discredited metric known as advertising value equivalency, commonly referred to as AVE. AVEs are dollar values assigned to public relations or earned coverage based on the cost to purchase an equivalent amount of space as advertising. There is and there will be no such thing as AVE for social media.

AVE is based on the notion that you can buy advertising that equates to what you have earned. In a social media world, comparing paid advertising to a blog, a tweet, or a Facebook thread is ludicrous. First of all, for most of the influential social media sites there is no equivalency, because they don't take advertising, or they don't have impressions or circulation figures. Sure there are 500 million people on Facebook. But how many really are seeing that photo album you published last week?

Secondly, unless you are an existing Facebook advertiser (or somehow have access to Facebook's internal data), the data is simply not available. Or take YouTube as an example. To compare a viral video like "Where the Hell Is Matt?" to an ad is like comparing a Warhol painting to velvet Elvis at the mall. Even if you were somehow able to purchase the 25,855,860 views (and counting) the video got, you'd still never earn the credibility that Stride Gum did by backing the project.

Finally, I question why anyone would want to count eyeballs and AVEs when they can count actual sales or outcomes. Elsewhere in this book you'll read many examples of companies that have measured hundreds of thousands of dollars in cost savings or revenue generated. Isn't that much more meaningful than AVEs? As for comparing different tactics, a far more effective way is to assess and compare their difference in impact on web traffic, click-throughs, registrations, and so forth.

CHAPTER 6

HOW TO USE NUMBERS TO GET CLOSER TO YOUR CUSTOMERS

"Do not get trapped into prior thoughts. It's perfectly okay to change your mind as you learn more."

—Dr. Donald A. Redelmeier

While in many ways social media has made all aspects of business more difficult, there is no denying that it has also brought with it enormous benefits in terms of our ability to get feedback from our customers and our marketplace. Before the advent of bulletin boards, wikis, and social networking sites, businesses had to rely on occasional market surveys to understand what their customers were thinking.

Now, listening in on customers' conversations is as easy as setting up a Google alert. With a few keystrokes, you can hear everything that anyone is saying in cyberspace about your brand, your products, and those of the competition. And, assuming you keep track of that feedback in some kind of a structured way, you can also perceive how the market reacts to your statements and actions over time and modify your business strategies appropriately.

To be clear, listening to the marketplace and listening to your specific customers require slightly different techniques, both of which are outlined in greater detail in the following pages.

LISTENING, LEARNING, AND RESPONDING TO THE MARKETPLACE

The first and arguably most difficult step in starting to listen to your marketplace is determining a universe to monitor. With some 600 blog posts and 36,500 tweets published every minute, it is very easy to get overwhelmed. Don't get hung up about getting everything—any given tool or search engine probably gets somewhere between 85 and 95 percent of what is out there. The important thing is not how *much* you're getting, but if you're getting *what matters to your business*. And, what matters to your business is what the customers in your market are talking about.

The good news is that it is also relatively easy to figure out what your marketplace is talking about. Any good web analytics program will give you statistics about what keywords people have used to find your site. Within Google AdWords there is a keyword suggestion tool that automatically suggests key words based on your market-place. Additionally, there are tools like www.wordtracker.com that can be used to even better define the specific words you should be searching for.

Set Up and Refine Your Search Strings

So your first step is to set up Google Alerts to search for those keywords. Monitor the results for a week or so to see if the terms you are using are collecting what you really want. For example, I set up an alert on my name, Katie Delahaye Paine. But 95 percent of what came up was about Delahaye the car, and had nothing to do with me. To deal with that I refined the search by putting the entire phrase "Katie Delahaye Paine" in quotes, and now I only get alerts when the entire phrase appears. Make sure you have set up alerts for all your competitors' names and brands in addition to the general terms describing your product or market areas.

Review and Track the Results

The first discovery you will make is that the vast majority of what comes in are either irrelevant mentions (such as wedding announcements, miscellaneous personal confessions, and such) or mentions that are relevant to some related search term that you are not interested in. By reading a few of the mentions you will get a sense of how much—probably upward of 70 percent—will need to be discarded.

The problem here is that computers are not very bright. Type in "SAS," for example, when looking for the analytical firm with that name, and a computer will give you everything from Scandinavian Airlines to San Antonio Shoes. When my company was analyzing all of HP's social media, half the mentions were about horsepower. So delete the duplicates and anything that is irrelevant.

Now set up an Excel spreadsheet to track items as they come in. Put the date the item appeared in the first column, the source in the next, the author in the third, and note the subject in the fourth column. If there are comments, links, trackbacks, or retweets for an item, they should be noted and tracked as well.

Verify Which Outlets Matter

At the end of a month or two, you'll have a list of those channels and outlets that most frequently mention you or your products or your market. If you want to further refine your list, you can calculate the ratio of comments to posts (it's called the Conversation Index) for each and rank them from highest (the most comments per post) to lowest (the fewest comments per post). Posts with more comments can generally be assumed to be of greater interest and greater influence to a greater number of people. Channels, outlets, and writers who get the most comments are usually more influential, and so you should pay particular attention to them.

Now you can either subscribe to or set up RSS feeds for each of those sources so that in the future they come directly into your inbox.

Determine What the Market Thinks of You and Your Competition: What Are Your Market Hot Buttons?

In addition to simple mentions of the brands and product lines in your marketplace, you should begin to get a sense of what hot buttons are emerging. Study the items to determine what issues (for example, price, value, delivery, availability) are the biggest concerns. Then determine how you are positioned on each one. Are you seen as a leader, follower, or laggard? Are you favorably positioned on those issues that are influencing buying decisions?

For example, at one point my company worked with a major consumer electronics firm that was suffering some market share loss in the small business arena. First we listened to what small business owners were saying about what drove their purchase decisions. In this case it was value for the money and the costs of ownership, driven primarily by the rapidly rising costs of supplies. It turned out that while our client was well positioned as an industry leader in innovation, it was seen by small business owners as having a higher cost of ownership than the competition. So those small business owners were buying from the competition for its perceived value for the money. As it turned out, leadership wasn't a big motivator at all in their purchase decisions. So we advised our client that it would continue to lose market share until it changed its positioning in the minds of small business owners.

Determine How You Are Positioned in the Marketplace versus the Competition, and Use That Knowledge to Gain Advantage

The most valuable information you glean from this exercise will not be what the market thinks of *your* brand or product but what it likes best and least about the *competition*. By finding out what the market thinks are your competition's strengths you can spot ways to improve your own products. By learning what the market sees as your competition's weaknesses, you can identify the best opportunities to gain an advantage.

Listening, Learning, and Responding to Your Customers

In addition to gaining a better understanding of the needs and issues of the marketplace, listening to social media conversations is also a great way to understand what is delighting or frustrating your customers. You can, in fact, use any of the common listening tools on the market, from Google Alerts to any number of sophisticated tools such as SAS social media analytics or Cymfony.

Again, the important component to any listening program is to have a way to organize and categorize the discussion. One way to do this is to use the 27 different types of conversations listed in Chapter 4. By focusing in on those specific comments that are expressing frustration, dismay, or dissatisfaction, you can easily identify areas for improvement.

You should also listen for conversations that provide insight into people's relationships with your brand as discussed in Chapter 4. By listening specifically for issues of trust and satisfaction, you can identify areas for improvement. In particular, analysis of structured product reviews on sites such as BizRate and Amazon can provide important indicators of future customer behaviors. Customers are much more likely to trust people like themselves when making a purchase decision. So, when customers are expressing happiness and satisfaction with a product, that conversation will weigh heavily on the purchase decisions of similar customers.

Turning Feelings into Numbers and Metrics

After you've collected and categorized the information, you need some way to quantify the data. The reality is that social media has no equivalent for impressions, because there are too many important blogs and media outlets that have no reliable readership numbers. There's also dubious value in attempting to equate the number of likes on Facebook or YouTube views with paid subscribers to *The Financial Times*, which means that what you really need to look at is percentages. Of all the conversations out there, what percent position your brand as a leader? Or of all the complaints being expressed out there, what percent mention you versus mention the competition?

As with any other measurement program, you need to establish benchmarks. Our recommendation is to use the competition as a benchmark, but measuring against yourself over time is also important.

For example, suppose you're launching a Go Green initiative and you intend to monitor the conversations to determine how you are perceived on the issue of sustainability. You'll want to start tracking those conversations well *before* the initiative is announced to establish a benchmark, and then continue tracking to see how soon the conversations on that theme pick up. You'll also want to track the competitive positioning to make sure that your voice is louder than that of your competition. But most important, you'll want to align your web analytics to see not just whether your customers are talking about your efforts, but whether they are taking action. Are they downloading information? Going to the sustainability section of your website? Purchasing your new green products? By looking at weekly web analytics in line with weekly conversation reports, you'll have a much better understanding of what is working and not working.

CHAPTER 7

MEASURING THE IMPACT OF EVENTS, SPONSORSHIPS, AND SPEAKING ENGAGEMENTS

"There is a lot of noise in the world. And there is a lot of idiosyncrasy. But there are also regularities and phenomena. And what the data is going to be able to do—if there's enough of it—is uncover, in the mess and the noise of the world, some lines of music that actually have harmony. It's there, somewhere."

—Esther Duflo

In an era where so much of business is conducted virtually, meeting customers, prospects, and other stakeholders IRL as they say, or "in real life," takes on a very different role than it did in the old days of sales calls and personal presentations. In today's world you need to measure and improve to keep costs down, to compare strategies, and to understand the true value of your events and sponsorships.

WHY EVENTS AND SPONSORSHIPS?

Generally speaking, organizations decide to participate in or sponsor an event with one of three goals in mind:

1. *Launch new products.* Events provide an opportunity to test drive a product or otherwise bring people in direct contact with the

brand. So a company might introduce a new product at a trade show so people can experience it in real life.

2. *Drive affinity between customers and the brand.* Sponsorship can demonstrate your brand's support for something the customer or prospect is passionate about. So a car dealership or restaurant might support a local school hockey team to show support for the community in hopes that the community will reciprocate and support the car dealer or restaurant. Rolex sponsors historic car races to support historic car enthusiasts, who tend to be an affluent demographic that can afford to buy Rolex products. Such sponsorships can build strong ties that result in passionate loyalty. To this day, I prefer Duracell batteries over other brands because the company was a huge supporter of a sailboat race I followed back in 1994.

3. *Reach new markets and customers.* To a certain extent there are events and shows in which *not* showing up says so much about your brand that a company has little choice other than to participate. Your presence at some events can establish your brand in a marketplace.

USE DATA TO SUPPORT YOUR EVENT DECISIONS

The one reason *not* to participate in an event or sponsorship is "because we always have." Whether you decide to participate or decide not to participate, you will need data to support your decision and to evaluate the efficacy of your participation. Without data, you're basing decisions on nothing more than hunches.

For example, whenever I get a request to speak at a conference, I consult a spreadsheet that compares data on all the speeches I've given in the last year. It shows:

- *Total attendees.* The number I can count in the audience or the actual attendee list. Never believe conference organizers; they always exaggerate.

- *Total views.* Actual number of people going to my speech page on the conference's website.
- *Total leads.* Number of business cards I bring home.
- *Site visits.* People who visit my own website, www.kdpaine.com, and move beyond the Speech archives.
- *Total contacts.* Total Contacts = Leads + Visits + Views
- *Costs.* Includes unreimbursed out-of-pocket costs as well as the cost of my time, less any compensation, speakers' fees, or reimbursements.

I use this spreadsheet to estimate the cost per lead, the number of leads per attendee, and the cost per contact. This information helps determine whether I should accept the invitation. Besides helping to make my speaking career more profitable, this form and process saves me hours of consideration and debate when a speaking invitation comes in.

Social Media Has Redefined the Concept of Events

As with most things in marketing today, social media has redefined events. While some organizations are opting for the "instant store" or airport or mall kiosk to get attention, an equal number of marketers are creating virtual events that bring like-minded people together around a cause, a game, or a memory. "Events" is a term that can now refer to an online fund-raiser or an in-person Twestival organized via Twitter. As we have seen with PR and other outreach methods, the companies that do this best are combining online and real time. What that means for measurement is that there are multiple dimensions to evaluate for any given event.

Events and the Relationships behind Brand Engagement: How Are People Involved with Your Brand?

This question brings us back to the importance of knowing something more than just how many eyeballs saw your brand, or how many people walked by your booth or display. A far more valuable measure is how many people are somehow engaged with your brand or your organization, and what is the nature and strength of that relationship?

In his seminal book *Lovemarks*, Kevin Roberts, CEO of Saatchi and Saatchi, describes how we develop relationships with the brands we love. Roberts argues that if a brand offers mystery, sensuality, and intimacy, it has the makings of a Lovemark. I argue that Lovemarks are all about building and nurturing relationships around a brand.

In fact, a 2004 study by Jack Morton Worldwide found that live event marketing—experiences in which consumers interact with products, brands, or brand ambassadors face-to-face—is among the most effective ways to influence coveted consumer audiences (www.accessmylibrary.com/coms2/summary_0286-19969873_ITM). The study, an online survey of 2,574 consumers between the ages of 13 and 65 in the top 25 U.S. markets, confirmed that this increasingly important marketing medium resonates strongly across all demographic and product categories.

So sponsorships, events, and other word-of-mouth programs have taken on a far more critical role than ever before. But it is no longer enough to simply measure the number of eyeballs reached by a bunch of banners or T-shirts. Today's savvy marketers are demanding much more than CPM numbers. They are looking to measure the relationships they are developing, both in terms of attitude change and in terms of buying and behaviors.

SEVEN STEPS TO MEASURE SPONSORSHIPS AND EVENTS

While measuring trade shows, events, and sponsorships are essentially three different things, the basic steps that need to be completed are similar and follow the seven steps described in Chapter 3.

Step 1: Define Your Objectives

As with any effort, you can't start to measure the success of an event until you know what success means for you. So the first thing to do is get consensus on goals and objectives for the event or sponsorship. If you are dealing with multiple audiences (consumer, corporate, institutional), then list those audiences and attach priority levels to each one.

In my experience, the great majority of companies cite product or corporate awareness as their primary objective. Other typical objectives include the following, each listed with typical measures.

Sell Products If you are just trying to sell products, then you will use basic measures such as:

- Gross sales per time period, before and after the event.
- Change in length of sales cycle.
- Change in intent to purchase.
- Change in traffic to website or brick-and-mortar locations.

Launch New Products This goal requires measures such as:

- Increase in market share.
- Increase in market penetration.
- Number of qualified leads for new product lines.
- Ratio of new to existing customers.
- Ratio of new to repeat visitors to website.
- Increase in depth or breadth of customer base.

Drive Affinity between Customers and the Brand If the event is designed to bring in new clients or improve relationships with old ones, then you will use measures such as:

- Increase in brand engagement.
- Increase in awareness.

- Increase in preference.
- Increase in exposure and dissemination for the company name, brand, or products.
- Increase in company or product knowledge among specific publics.

Reach New Markets and Customers If you are attending shows to get leads, build fan bases, and/or generate attendees, you will use measures such as:

- Increase in new market-specific sales leads.
- Increase in awareness or preference or intent to purchase in the new market.
- Increase in mindshare.

Step 2: Determine Your Measurable Criteria of Success

Once you've agreed upon your objectives, establish the specific criteria of success that you will measure. If your objective is awareness, a criterion might be the percentage increase of unaided awareness of brand or product. If your objective is to sell product, your criterion might be the incremental sales or traffic to local dealers after a particular PR or promotional program took place.

Consider using metrics that best reflect the health of your business or that best represent customer characteristics that most affect your business, including:

- Percent of attendees more likely to purchase.
- Percent of attendees remembering the brand.
- Number of qualified sales leads generated.
- Conversion rate of attendees.
- Total potential sales (number of attendees x conversion rate x average sale).
- For press events: Number of key editors and analysts attending.

- Percent of attendees writing on or quoted on a particular issue.
- Total exposure of key messages in resulting press.
- Number of tweets or retweets of speeches or presentations.
- Percent conversion from a specific event website to a corporate site.

To a certain extent, your choice of criteria is dependent on the type of event you are evaluating. If the customer experience you are measuring takes place at a trade show or exhibit booth, you might choose as a key criterion the percentage of new visitors or the cost-per-minute spent with a client in the booth. If the experience takes place at an event such as a concert, count how many people were exposed to your brand or the brand experience you were offering. Don't trust the promoter's numbers; do your own counting. I often follow up with a survey to see if attendees remember the brand.

Step 3: Decide Upon Your Benchmarks

The key point to remember about any evaluation program is that measurement is a comparative tool: You need to compare one set of results to something else. The most meaningful comparisons are between different events or between you and competing sponsors at one event.

Define your benchmarks based on the decisions you need to make. Are you comparing show to show or show vs. direct mail vs. Facebook? Are you taking into account different geographies or different time frames? Are you weighing different types of sponsorships: sailing vs. tennis or sports vs. community?

Step 4: Select a Measurement Tool

In our opinion, the most reliable way to measure relationships with your customers is to conduct an in-depth phone survey using the

Grunig Relationship Survey (see Chapter 4 and Appendix 1). This instrument has been thoroughly tested and shown to be an extremely effective measure of how customers perceive their relationships with an organization. The Grunig Relationship Survey includes a number of statements with which respondents are asked if they agree or disagree. Typical statements include:

- This organization treats people like me fairly and justly.
- This organization can be relied on to keep its promises.
- I believe that this organization takes the opinions of people like me into account when making decisions.
- I feel very confident about this organization's skills.

Online surveys are most organization's first choice these days. While they do suffer from self-selecting samples, the advantages of low cost and quick turnaround are hard to beat. They are particularly effective in measuring relationships with members of an organization that are all on a mailing list or Listserv of some sort (Chapter 9).

If you are evaluating whether an event changed perceptions about your brand, most people would think about doing some kind of on-site survey, but that's probably the *last* thing you should do. By far, the most valuable assessment can be derived from a post-show survey that will provide clear insights into visitors' takeaways—their longer-term perceptions and memories. These are much more effectively gathered after the event via an online survey.

My company has conducted numerous trade show surveys, both on-site and after events, with samples composed of people who actually visit a booth. Typically, about 20 percent of people surveyed (and, remember, these are people who had to be in the booth for us to get their names) do not recall visiting the booth at all. We find that whatever people do remember after the show is of greater value than their on-site responses, when they are often most concerned about their sore feet.

For example, data from post-show surveys is far more revealing and reliable about purchase intent. If you ask event attendees at a show if they are likely to purchase a product, chances are they'll say yes just to make the interviewer happy. But if you call after the fact and ask if they have purchased or intend to purchase, the response is far more likely to reflect reality. Remember, however, that in event measurement time is of the essence. You need the data in time to make decisions, and typically those decisions are made fairly quickly after an event is concluded.

An alternative to the on-site or post-show survey is to closely track website traffic before, during, and after an event to determine if there are any significant changes as a result of the event. Or, if you are a consumer packaged-goods company, you can use scanning data to track sales impact. As an example, Colgate Palmolive sponsored the Starlight Starbright Children's Foundation and promoted it in point-of-sale communications for several specific brands. It then tracked the sell-through of those brands after the sponsorship was launched. As it turns out, the sponsorship was very effective for boosting sales of some of its brands but had little impact on others.

In another example, the Humane Society used a simple "Donate $1" to judge the effectiveness of a "Cute Puppy Photo Contest" on Flickr and raised some $650,000. But to correlate events to sales or donations requires close coordination between your web analytics and event planning.

An alternative made possible by the real-time world of social media is to create a hashtag (a nickname for your event preceded by the # sign) to help you search and track any and all references to the event. Then you can follow the real-time comments on Twitter and other social networking sites to see how people perceive your brand or the event.

Step 5: Define Your Specific Metrics

If your goal is to change people's opinions about you—to convince them that you are in the market, or back in the market, or doing better than your competition—then your metrics will be:

- Percent change in perceptions.
- Percent change in awareness.
- Percent increase in preference.
- Percent of attendees likely to purchase.

If your goal is to sell stuff, your metrics might concern greater efficiency as measured by:

- *Cost per contact.* Event budget divided by the number of people who had the opportunity to see your brand, whether in the booth, via other media, on Twitter, or wherever.
- *Cost per lead.* Event budget divided by the number of raw leads you collect.
- *Cost per qualified lead.* Event budget divided by the number of qualified leads.
- *Cost per customer acquisition.* Event budget divided by the number of actual customers acquired from the event.
- *Cost per minute spent with prospect.* This is a particularly useful metric if you are comparing events to direct sales activities. What does it cost you to spend time with a prospect at a show versus the cost of a sales call (typically north of $300)? You'll need to count the number of contacts or demos your booth staff make and determine an average amount of time per demo. So, for example, suppose you do 1,000 demos and your budget is $50,000 for the show. Then the cost per demo would be $50. If each demo takes 10 minutes you have generated 10,000 customer contact minutes at a cost of $5 per customer contact minute.
  - You can then compare this metric to that for an advertisement or a sales call as follows: Suppose you develop and purchase an ad for $100,000, and it reaches an audience of 50,000

people. That's $2 per person reached. Suppose they each spend 15 seconds reading the ad, then the cost is $8 per customer contact minute. Now suppose it costs you $500 to get a sales-person in front of a prospective customer for a five-minute sales call. Then a sales call works out to $100 per customer contact minute, clearly not much of a bargain compared to the ad and the event.

- *Length of sales cycle.* Use your customer relationship management (CRM) system to track the length of the sales cycle for attendees versus nonattendees of the event to see if the event results in faster sales. If you survey your attendees afterward to determine whether they plan to purchase your products and how soon, you can compare the results show-by-show to your overall company average.

Step 6: Choose a Measurement Tool

Counting Tools

- *A clicker.* Sometimes the easiest thing to do is to just stand in the booth and count bodies. Use a regular clicker and count the average number of people in the booth at the top of the hour. Or, repeat at random times throughout the day to get an average.
- *Categorization.* It helps to categorize event attendees by the degree to which they are engaged in your event. Are they just looking at your signage, or are they actually entering the booth and having a conversation? What percentage of attendees ends up as leads?

Survey Tools

- We recommend post-show electronic surveys (SurveyMonkey or Benchpoint) because they will test what people ultimately remember about the event experience, not just their on-site reactions.

Sales Tracking Tools

- You need a database to enter leads and track them through the sales process, be it a simple contact manager like the one in Outlook, or some form of CRM system like SalesForce or FileMaker.

Web Analytic Tools

- Whether you're an e-commerce company or just drive people to your website for more information, you need to determine whether your activities at the show are helping engage your potential customers. Google Analytics works just fine, but if you're already using something like Omniture or WebTrends it's even better. Create a unique URL for your event to which all event-related traffic is directed. You can then see how much traffic comes into that specific URL and where it goes once people are done on that page. Do they leave your site completely, or do they go elsewhere on your site for information about your products or company?

Content Analysis Tools

- If you want to track what people say about your event, both before and afterward, you will want to scan social as well as traditional media. Assuming you have used a hashtag on Twitter, you will be able to easily track conversations there. You can set up Google Alerts or use your existing clipping service, but make sure you begin tracking the buzz as soon as you put your marketing materials out there.
- Separate out your self-manufactured buzz (tweets, Facebook page, blogs, SlideShare, etc.) from the content that other people have put out there. Note the medium, the data, the author, and, if possible, the source. Was it from a speaker, an attendee, or a competitor?

- You'll want to analyze all the content for the following elements:
  - *Product mentions.* Did the products you featured at the show appear in the conversations? Did they show up more prominently or visibly than the competitions' products?
  - *Messaging/positioning.* Do the conversations position you in the marketplace the way you want to be positioned?
  - *Key messages.* Do they appear at all? If so, are they fully communicated, or only partially, or—God forbid—inaccurately repeated? Were attendees so engaged that they amplified your messages?
  - *Quotes.* Did you have thought leaders speaking at the event? Were they followed? Were they retweeted? Are they amplifying your key messages?
  - *Visibility and prominence.* Were your announcements covered in headlines or were you a minor mention? Did photos appear?

Step 7: Analyze Your Results and Use Them to Make Your Events More Effective

Using a combination of your web analytics and CRM system you should be able to get a good profile of who was at your event and what they did as a result. If you do use a follow-up survey, try to get as much information as possible from visitors as to what made them come, what was memorable, and what they plan to do with the information they gleaned.

Analyze and learn from the survey results. Determine what specific elements engaged them with your brand. What specific part of your marketing program helped them decide to attend? What elements were most memorable?

Don't just compare events; look at the big picture. Are events the most efficient way to get your message across or to get new leads? Compare online events to real-life events.

HOW TO CALCULATE ROI FOR A BOOTH AT AN EVENT: WAS IT WORTH THE TIME AND RESOURCES?

It is fairly straightforward to determine your return on an event. First, ask your sales and accounting departments for figures on the average profit margin on a sale and the total cost to attend the event. Then determine how many people visited the booth and conduct a post-show survey of all the leads collected in your booth. Ask respondents if they intend to purchase, when they intend to purchase, and how much they intend to spend. Be clear that you are measuring intentions not actual purchases.

Now use this data to calculate ROI. Here's how it works: If 50 percent of respondents indicate that they intend to purchase and you know that 1,000 people visited your booth, that means that 500 people intend to purchase something from your organization. If, on average, the respondents indicate that they each plan to spend $1,000 on your products or services at some point in the next six months, then you can project approximately $500,000 in sales from the show. Now, to calculate the actual return you need to multiply that $500,000 by your average profit margin on a sale (revenue minus cost of goods sold). So if your profit margin is 50 percent, you can then assume that the actual revenue from the show will be $250,000. Now take the show's expenses—including the booth, staff time, travel, and so forth—and subtract them from that $250,000 and you will have the net ROI for your event.

Don't forget to include accurate costs of attending. Travel budgets are severely restricted these days and a small change in the price of a ticket can make a big difference.

It's important to look beyond simple quantitative data, especially if your objective is exposure, to assess the quality of your communications. Do attendees remember being in your booth? Did they even know you were a sponsor? Did they remember your brand, and the brand benefits or brand positioning you were trying to convey? Did they leave more likely to purchase or to recommend?

When a company clearly defines its objectives, it becomes a relatively simple matter to define a set of criteria against which to measure the company's relationships with its constituencies in different events. Then it is possible to compare and contrast results consistently across a number of different events to ensure that the company has the most effective sponsorship program possible.

REAL-LIFE EVENT MEASUREMENT STORIES

The Case of the Unfocused Auto Manufacturer

I met with a major auto manufacturer that wanted to measure the effectiveness of different sponsorships. It was spending many millions of dollars sponsoring car races, golf tournaments, antique car auctions, and a variety of other events. I asked the assembled executives what they were trying to achieve by these efforts. The first response was essentially: "We are a major sponsor of these types of events." Finally, after about two hours of discussion, we agreed that the business objective was to drive potential customers into dealer showrooms.

We began a series of surveys at each event to determine first if the attendees remembered the sponsors and second if they were more or less likely to test drive and/or buy the auto manufacturer's cars. We collected names at the event itself and called attendees two weeks after the event. Our results showed that, on average, 50 percent of all attendees were more likely to test drive one of the sponsor's vehicles after attending the event. After we had measured several events, we were able to compare and contrast the cost effectiveness (dollars per person reached) of different events. See Figure 7.1.

Figure 7.1

Comparing events with projected ROI. Event results varied greatly.

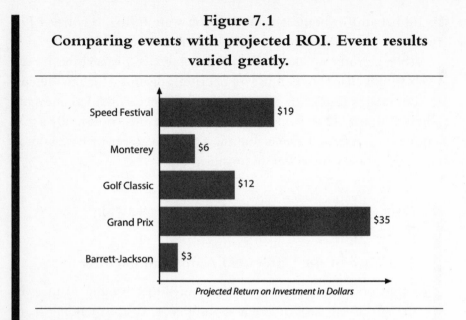

Projected Return on Investment in Dollars

These results led the auto manufacturer to alter its sponsorship strategies dramatically and focus more on golf and antique car events rather than traditional car races. It also enabled the sponsor to better understand the ROI from each event. By looking at the percentage of people more likely to go to a dealership, it could determine the number of potential buyers. By subtracting the cost of the sponsorship from the projected number of car sales and the profit, it determined a projected ROI from the event.

Country Music Television Tunes In to Its Viewers

Country Music Television (CMT) had a program of sponsoring country music concerts in Walmart parking lots. The concerts would move from location to location in tractor trailers. Prior to getting in touch with me, CMT had measured results by asking the truck drivers how many people showed up. Realizing that this might not be the most accurate methodology, it contracted with my company to design a measurement program for these events.

CMT's stated purpose was to convince attendees to call their local cable company and request CMT, or to take some other action on behalf of CMT. We agreed with CMT that the common criterion against which we should measure all events was an ad-hoc measure we called "level of engagement." This was defined as the average response of attendees, on a scale of 1 to 5, when asked how much the parking lot event affected their relationship with CMT. We further defined success as an increase in the percentage of people willing to take action on behalf of CMT. A sweatshirt giveaway was included at the events to collect names and addresses of attendees. We surveyed a sample of these people by phone two weeks after the event.

Our surveys showed that 93 percent of attendees were willing to take some action and 89 percent were willing to make a phone call to their local cable company. We then compared results between different events in different cities so CMT could determine where to expand the program the following year.

CHAPTER 8

HOW TO MEASURE INFLUENCERS AND THOUGHT LEADERSHIP

"Dominant coalitions tend to value and support communicators who first demonstrate their worth."

—David Dozier

In the good old days, influencers were recognized leaders in business, media, Wall Street, or academia. Today, an influencer can be anyone who knows something about your product, your market, or your business. It can be someone with 10,000 followers on Twitter or 500 friends on Facebook. All that matters is whether they recommend your product or service.

NEW INFLUENCERS, NEW THOUGHT LEADERS, NEW RELATIONSHIPS

It used to be that a good communications program functioned like a food chain. You would educate key spokespeople and influencers on your message, and, assuming it was a credible message, it flowed down through the chain of media and ultimately reached your publics through a variety of credible sources. This top-down process of message control seemed reasonable, but was probably only a convenient illusion. Social media has proved it wrong and officially signed its death certificate.

Today, to mangle the metaphor a bit, the minnows are feeding on the sharks. Influence is no longer held by one large analyst firm or even a single credible individual, but rather resides in whatever community, Facebook page, or Twitter list that is talking about your marketplace. The proliferation of low- or no-cost tools to create communities has sparked a proliferation of highly specialized groups of people that are interested in very narrow topics. These groups are essentially newsgroups that have come of age: They are the former teenagers who have moved out of their parents' basements and now own the party houses. Whether it's small farmers, fans of a particular product, or parents of children with a specific disease, there's now a group for it. And that group has members and the members have friends and all of them can influence your market and your market share.

I used to tell people to treat bloggers like influential industry analysts. Now I advise the opposite: Treat industry analysts just like you would a blogger. That is, engage in a conversation. Not in a "here's the message I'm shoving down your throat" way, but rather, a two-way dialog that focuses on what the individual has been blogging about. Talk with the blogger about something that you know he is interested in—just as you'd woo an interesting person at a cocktail party. Woe to those who haven't devoted some serious time to determine what the blogger's hot buttons are. Not only do you risk annoying the blogger, but you might be labeled as a spammer. And the blogger is likely to tell all his friends to shun you as well.

So throw out all your old assumptions and put in place a measurement and evaluation program for your influentials. Don't get me wrong, the thought leaders, early adopters, industry analysts, financial analysts, key customers, academics, and political leadership still play an enormous role in shaping opinion. The difference is that they can no longer be seduced with a corporate subscription to their services.

Many of them have simply left to start their own consultancies; others are so fiercely independent that they automatically shun any hint of complicity with an organization.

So let's be specific in our definitions. In every industry, there are influential figures who write more, say more, and speak in public more. These are the people who others turn to for advice and recommendations. In hair care, it's the hairstylists. In high tech, it's the key industry consultants. In automobiles, it's the car enthusiasts. Every industry has them, and if you don't have a good relationship with them, it will be very hard for your organization, your products, or your job to survive.

How to Build a Custom List of the Top 100 Influencers in Your Marketplace

You can probably name the 25 or so most important influencers in your marketplace already. The problem this next section will solve is how to determine all the *other* people who may be influencing purchasing decisions within your industry. It may seem to be a very cool thing to be able to tap into the entire social media universe to hear what people are saying about you. And it is. But 90 percent of what you find is likely to be noise. So how do you sort out the noise from who and what matters?

First, you need to understand that who and what matters is very specific to your target audiences. NPR's Planet Money blog may be hugely influential to business, but if you're selling video games to teenagers, then T.E.E.N. Diaries blog is far more important. If you are a consumer goods company selling toilet paper, then product management may need to focus on mommy bloggers, while corporate communications might be far more concerned with environmental-action.org.

Here's how to build your own list of the top 100 who matter in your marketplace.

***Step 1: Search for Blogs That Mention You or Your Marketplace Most
Frequently*** If you are already using a listening tool like SM2, Google
News, or Radian6, it very probably has an algorithm built in that
purports to determine key influencers. In reality, it's just counting
up the number of times people write about your brand or your
marketplace. Still, it's not a bad place to start. The most important
thing is to look for more than just your brand. Make sure you are
searching for the competition and that you include the entire market
space that you are in or want to be in.

You'll need three to six months worth of data to start. Capture the
source of a mention and the number of times that source has written
about your brand and/or the competition or the market space you are
in. If you're using Google News or some other free source, you'll need
to do searches on a regular basis. Once a day use Google Feedfetcher
or just manually collect everything that Google finds about you and
put it into an Excel spreadsheet. Be sure you:

- Delete the duplicates and anything that is irrelevant. Watch out
  for faux blogs that exist only to push coupons or ads on unsus-
  pecting readers. Check the comments section and the writer's
  authority and history to make sure there's a real person behind
  the blog.
- Put the date in the first column, the source in the next,
  the author in the third, and note the subject in the fourth
  column.
- Then note number of comments for each one.

Step 2: Verify That the Blogs and Bloggers Are Actually Important
At the end of six months you'll have a list of those blogs that
mention you or your marketplace most frequently. Rank them in
terms of numbers of mentions—first for your brands, then for the
competition. Pare the list down to 100. Now analyze those publications to determine which sources their editors, bloggers, or
reporters turn to for advice and information. Use a database or

spreadsheet to record—for every article about you, your industry, or your competition—the name of the publication, the name of the reporter, and the names of everyone quoted. This will give you a list of the most frequently quoted sources. Also record several other details about each item:

- Was it entirely about you or your industry or category?
- Did the influencer quoted refer directly to your organization, or was the quote about someone else?
- And finally, did the article and/or quote contain one or more of your key messages?

Now, take the 100 sources who have mentioned you most frequently and any others you have identified as important and run each through Blog Grader and Twitalyzer and rank them in order of their scores. This will give you an indicator of the reach of the individual blogger. Now calculate the Conversation Index for each one (that's the ratio of comments to posts). Rank them from highest (the most comments per post) to lowest (the fewest comments per post).

Add the three ranks (the ranks, not the scores) together and sort them from high to low. Get online and check the top 50 to verify that they really are relevant to your brand and your market or your client.

Now you've got a list that is truly yours and truly valuable. Keep it that way by repeating this process on a biannual basis.

How to Measure Your Relationships with Your Influencers

As with journalists, the ultimate measure of a successful relationship with analysts and influencers is whether they recommend your product, service, or company to reporters, editors, investors, and customers. The methodology for measuring your results is similar to that for measuring the media with one key exception: Periodically assessing the health of your relationships with them is absolutely critical, because understanding what they *think* about you is just as important as understanding what they *write* about you.

Here's an example of how it can benefit a business. The beauty care division of a major consumer packaged goods company was trying to figure out how to improve its overall awareness and preference with its target customers: women between the ages of 18 and 35. It knew that this audience read the top 15 beauty magazines for advice, but it wasn't sure how to influence those publications. My firm conducted a share-of-ink study to determine how much coverage each of our client's product categories (hair care, facial care, sunscreen, etc.) received during the course of the year. We looked at all the articles about those products and quickly established that hair stylists and salon owners were most frequently quoted.

This media analysis effort yielded a valuable database that allowed our client to spot trends in product recommendations, and tie those recommendations to promotional efforts. Our client could also establish its share of recommendations against other firms in the industry. Our client made an effort to reach out to the most-quoted groups, both in industry-specific trade publications and with events and specially tailored programs. The final, ideal result would be to tie the firm's share of recommendations to market share data.

Let's address the elements of influencer measurement one at a time using the steps introduced in Chapter 3 as a guide.

Step 1: Define Your Goals

Influencer or analyst relations (AR) programs are typically developed with the ultimate goal of getting the analyst to recommend your product or at least to defend it from competitive attacks. But AR programs are also essential to any successful entry into a new marketplace and to any change of positioning your organization may be attempting.

So define a list of measurable objectives for your influencer outreach program.

Step 2: Define Your Audience

The more specifically you can define your audience the better. In Chapter 3, you defined what your target audiences were for all of your marketing programs. In this exercise you will need to define which specific influencer groups you are targeting. Typical influencer groups might include:

- Government officials
- Bloggers
- Nongovernmental organizations
- Professors and academic experts
- Investment analysts
- Technology analysts
- Market analysts
- Anyone else quoted frequently in national media

Step 3: Define Your Benchmark

Measurement is a comparative tool, so you need to be clear about who or what you are comparing your results to. Is your program designed to pit your CEO *mano a mano* against the CEO of a rival company for share of quotes? Or are you trying to get industry influencers to love your company more than that upstart across the street? In either case you need to be clear about the benchmarks you are trying to reach, and what you will be comparing your success against.

With opinion leaders it is particularly important to compare your organization to your peers and competitors, since all of you will be pitching competing messages and stories to the same opinion leaders. Be sure to ask them how your organization ranks in their minds relative to others in the industry.

Step 4: Define Your Key Performance Indicators

The key performance indicators by which to judge your influencer relations program should include one or more of the following (listed in order of preference):

- Percent increase in Grunig Relationship Survey scores, specifically in the areas of trust, commitment, satisfaction, and exchange versus communal relationships. (See Chapter 4 and Appendix 1.)
- Percent increase in share of recommendations.
- Percent increase in share of desired positioning.
- Percent increase in share of desirable quotes.
- Percent increase in coverage containing desirable quotes from key influencers.

Step 5: Select Your Measurement Tool

Tools to measure influencer relations range from the simple to the highly complex, and accuracy increases accordingly. At the most basic level you can use Excel or Access to track what key influencers are saying and writing about you in the media. You can also use your web analytics program to determine how much traffic is coming from your key influencers' sites.

A slightly more labor intensive but far more important tool is a content analysis of all of your media mentions to determine if they are saying or writing what you want them to. On a weekly or monthly basis collect all the items referencing you and the organizations against which you are benchmarking. Analyze them for the number and nature of the quotes.

To truly get the most useful data about your key influencers I recommend regular biannual relationship surveys, conducted by phone or e-mail. The purpose is to determine the extent to which these influencers understand your strategies and mission, the extent to which they believe in your management's ability, and their overall image of—and trust in—your organization. We recommend developing a standard survey instrument based on the Grunig Relationship Survey. (See Appendix 1.)

Typical questions would be: Do you agree or disagree with the following statements?

- This organization has the ability to accomplish what it says it will do.
- In dealing with people like me, this organization has a tendency to throw its weight around.
- I would rather work together with this organization than not.
- Most people enjoy dealing with this organization.

It is also important to integrate your research with other developments within your organization. Here's an example: Tracy Eiler, formerly at Business Objects (now SAP), had been tracking analyst relations for a number of years. When budgets got tight a few years ago, she was forced to eliminate a position that was specifically charged with maintaining analyst relations. The following reporting period saw a dramatic decline in how the analyst community viewed Business Objects, particularly on the subject of responsiveness. Without the extra person, the company just couldn't be as responsive as it had been in the past. She charted the drop and subsequent decline in quotes in the media, presented the results to her boss, and the position was reestablished.

Tracking analysts can also help identify new opportunities for influence. At one time a few years ago, we were tracking a core list of key analysts that a major computer company had established. As it turned out, some of the members of that list were seldom quoted, and from time to time there were quotes from new names. By providing our client with an update of active influencers each month, we were able to continuously improve the effectiveness of the analyst relations effort.

The final steps for thought leader measurement follow steps six and seven as outlined in Chapter 3.

CASE STUDY: INFLUENCING SALES BY TARGETING KEY INFLUENCERS

Kami Huyse's 2007 Journey to Atlantis social media campaign for SeaWorld San Antonio has become a classic case study on how to use social media to target key influencers (http://overtonecomm.blogspot.com/2008/04/case-study-roi-of-social-media-campaign.html). SeaWorld wanted to launch its new Journey to Atlantis roller coaster with the help of buzz from influentials in the coaster community. So it identified 22 coaster enthusiast blogs and created content to suit their needs. Video and photos of the coaster and its construction were posted on sites like YouTube and Flickr. Coaster enthusiasts and bloggers were invited to attend the media launch day and be among the first to ride the coaster.

Results showed impressive success: 12 of the 22 blogs covered the ride, and the campaign received 50 links from unique websites, 30 of which were from coaster enthusiast sites. The American Coaster Enthusiasts group brought 30 of its members to ride the coaster on media day. An exit survey showed that the cost per impression for the social media campaign was $0.22, versus $1.00 for television. The online efforts represented more than $2.6 million in revenue.

CASE STUDY: NEW HAMPSHIRE INFLUENCES THE INFLUENCERS TO CHANGE ITS POLITICAL IMAGE

Tracking influencers and carefully tailoring your messages to them can have a major impact on reputation. One study of New Hampshire's reputation in the media revealed that it appeared to be populated by flannel-shirted hicks, citizens who didn't deserve their unusual political influence as voters in the first-in-the-nation presidential primary.

A group of state leaders headed by former governor Hugh Gregg decided they needed to change this perception. The New Hampshire Political Library (NHPL), which Gregg founded, conducted a detailed media analysis of New Hampshire's presidential primary coverage. After reading and analyzing some 3,000 articles that referred to the State of New Hampshire's attributes and failings, they had a list of the reporters and journalists who were most likely to visit or write about the state. Additionally, they were able to isolate two dozen influencers who journalists regularly went to for information about the state or the primary.

They then provided those influencers with facts and figures about the state, such as:

- New Hampshire has the highest per capita number of high-tech jobs in the country.
- There are over 200 languages spoken in the Manchester school system.
- New Hampshire citizens participate in politics with greater frequency than citizens of any other state in the union: 75 percent have voted in the primary, 74 percent have watched a debate or have otherwise paid attention, and 13 percent have attended an event.
- One in 10 New Hampshire residents has shaken the hand of a candidate.

The NHPL also worked with the leaders of both political parties (who were on the list of top influencers) to change candidates' photo opportunity venues. Prior to the 2000 election

(continued)

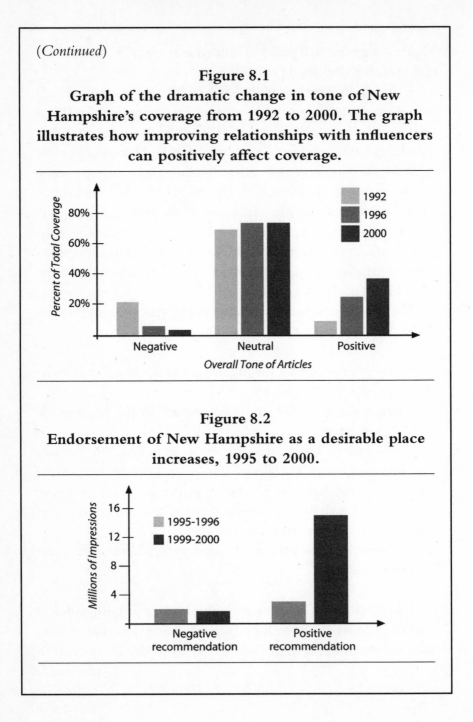

(*Continued*)

Figure 8.1
Graph of the dramatic change in tone of New Hampshire's coverage from 1992 to 2000. The graph illustrates how improving relationships with influencers can positively affect coverage.

Figure 8.2
Endorsement of New Hampshire as a desirable place increases, 1995 to 2000.

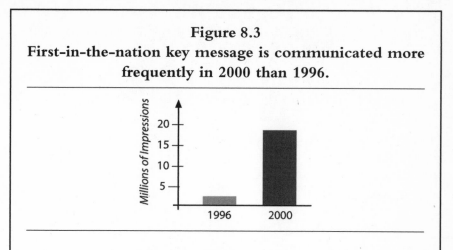

Figure 8.3
First-in-the-nation key message is communicated more frequently in 2000 than 1996.

year, most presidential candidates' photos had been staged around maple trees and in diners. As a result of the efforts of NHPL, most of the photo opportunities in 2000 occurred in high-tech factories and manufacturing venues.

As a result of all these efforts, the overall tone of coverage dramatically shifted (see Figure 8.1). Journalists who once had described New Hampshire citizens as "backward," "quirky," or "persnickety" were now saying that the state deserved the primary because of its citizens' intense level of political engagement (see Figures 8.2 and 8.3). Further analysis showed that the messages were frequently communicated in quotations from influencers identified in the earlier study (Gittell and Gottlob, 2001).

CHAPTER 9

MEASURING RELATIONSHIPS WITH YOUR LOCAL COMMUNITY

"All business in a democratic society begins with public permission and exists by public approval."

—Arthur Page

Given the speed with which news, crises, and complaints can travel, public approval can be granted or withdrawn at a moment's notice. So today it is more important than ever to understand and measure and improve your relationships with your local community.

WHO ARE YOUR NEIGHBORS AND WHY ARE THEY IMPORTANT?

Social media has introduced an entirely new definition of community. Communities today are not necessarily those individuals and organizations in close physical proximity to your business. Communities can be virtual and consist of any group of stakeholders that exerts influence over your business. This includes your own internal communities of customers, vendors, and partners, as well as external advocates, nongovernmental organizations, and any other community with which you have a relationship.

How Do Good or Bad Relationships Influence Your Organization?

The short answer is that you ignore your communities at your peril. When Amazon ignored its community of Kindle users, a firestorm erupted over its deletion of certain books to which it didn't have legal distribution rights. Amazon was, legally, making the correct move, but the community didn't care; it felt that Amazon had broken its promise to them. To regain the lost trust of the community required an abject apology and admission of wrongdoing from Amazon's CEO.

On the other hand, communities with which you have good relationships can defend you in a crisis. When Shamu the whale killed its trainer at SeaWorld, the watchdog group People for the Ethical Treatment of Animals (PETA) began a fierce "free all whales" Facebook campaign against SeaWorld. However, because SeaWorld had long nurtured its community on Facebook, the PETA voices were quickly drowned out by SeaWorld fans.

Who and What Is Most Important to Measure?

Most organizations focus most of their PR efforts on groups they consider to be their key publics, for instance, their customers, financial analysts, and maybe the media. Not until there is picketing at the gates do they wake up and realize that there are other publics they need to get permission and approval from. Today, consumers, employees, and other stakeholders simply expect any organization they do business with to have some sort of corporate social responsibility (CSR) or local community outreach program in place. Unfortunately, if all the organization does is to designate someone to do a few speeches at the Rotary Club, some United Way activities, and a flurry of self-congratulatory press releases, it will have accomplished very little. And without good metrics in place the organization is apt to assume that its relationships with the neighbors are just fine, thank you. It's not until a permit is denied, a key vote is lost, or the protesters are back at the gates that someone wonders whether all that time and money spent on the community relations department was worth anything. That's why it is important to maintain ongoing assessment of your relationships with your publics, so you know where you stand, and what works and what doesn't.

Many organizations think that by saying the right things and controlling their messages they can preserve their image as a good place to work or as a good neighbor. But today, with millions of bloggers and Twitterers out and about with their Flip video cameras and cell phone cameras, messages cannot be contained. Anyone with a grudge or an agenda can poke holes in a carefully crafted image. And while the public still doesn't expect organizations to be fully accessible, if they can't easily contact you, then they'll take their grievances to the Twitterverse or blogosphere in a heartbeat. And a few bloggers can spiral into an army of angry neighbors in a matter of days.

In their book, *Excellent Public Relations and Effective Organizations*, James E. Grunig, Larissa A. Grunig, and David M. Dozier showed that the best relationships are fostered by two-way, synchronous relations between organizations and their publics, rather than the old-school asynchronous message-pushing style (Grunig, Grunig, & Dozier, 2002). With good research, any organization can assess exactly where its relationships are weakest and then use two-way communications to improve them.

SEVEN STEPS TO MEASURING RELATIONSHIPS WITH YOUR COMMUNITIES AND NEIGHBORS

Measurement of your relationships with your communities follows the seven steps outlined in Chapter 3.

Step 1: Agree upon Solid Measurable Goals That Are Tied to the Bottom Line

Like measuring any other business relationship, gauging the strength or weakness of your reputation among your greater community of stakeholders must start with a clear goal. Getting consensus around the objectives for your program is a necessity, especially because many accounting types look upon corporate social responsibility and community relations as a costly add-on to normal operations. In fact, the opposite is usually the case: Doing charitable work in your communities is frequently a way to lower recruiting costs, reduce legal bills, and raise the total return to your shareholders. So Step 1 is really to identify the problem you're trying to solve and what the organization will look like assuming you succeed.

Step 2: Define Your Publics

Next, define your community and your publics. Include all the various stakeholders that play a role in your success, because in this new hyperconnected world there is no way to isolate your actions or your relationships. Start with a list of all the publics you are trying to influence. Include elected and appointed officials, heads of local special interest groups, and anyone else who might influence public perceptions of your organization. Include what James Grunig and Fred Repper call active publics and passive publics (Grunig and Repper, 1992), as well as anyone who can do you either harm or good. These key stakeholders are your audience.

One word of caution: Community is really much too general a term for our purpose here; the community is often made up of very disparate elements. For instance, I live in the little town of Durham, New Hampshire, home to some 7,500 other souls. Durham is also the home of the University of New Hampshire, and many of my fellow community members attend the university. Although technically I am a part of the Durham community, there are a great many other members of the community with whom I have very little in common. These include the ones who drink excessive quantities of beer, burn their mattresses in the street, and then pass out on fraternity lawns, for example. Just because they are students doesn't mean that their votes or their opinions are any less worthy of attention; they just need a slightly different type of attention. If they're on your list of key stakeholders, they can either help or hurt your cause. Itemize exactly how a good relationship helps your reputation and how a bad relationship threatens your reputation. See Figure 9.1.

Step 3: Who or What Are Your Benchmarks?

Since measurement is a comparison tool, you will need to compare the strength of your community relations to something or someone else. It could be to other communities, such as other towns where you may have a plant or office. Better yet, compare yourself to peer organizations of similar size and reputation within the same community. For example, when we studied the local reputation of a major corporation in Minneapolis, we chose to compare against a department store and a food producer, both of which were comparably charitable and comparably visible in the community. In another example, when an international airline wanted to gauge its relationship with the local media, we compared local media coverage to coverage of the same airline in other cities around the country.

One of the problems in finding another organization with which to compare your results is that so many organizations are the only game in town. Ordinarily, you'd like to be able to benchmark against your direct competition, but the chances of having a competing company or organization in the same neighborhood are fairly slim. In my town of Durham, for example, the University of New Hampshire is by far the dominant institution.

To find an appropriate benchmark in these cases you may need to go outside your local community and team up with your peers at comparable organizations in comparable communities elsewhere.

Figure 9.1
Community influencers, and how a good or bad relationship with each group impacts your organization.

Influencer	Impact or Benefit
Elected officials	Can withhold or grant permission to expand/build
Official wannabes and candidates	Can make a campaign issue out of your plans
Customers	Contribute to revenue
Noncustomers	Potential customers, potential employees
NGOs	Influence elected officials, have the ear of the local media
Town staff	Can create or reduce paper work, grant approvals
Local radio and TV reporters	Primary source of news for local community
Local print reporters	Read by the influentials, source of opinions
Senior citizens	Votes, volunteers
Students	Votes, volunteers, future employees, future customers
Academics	Opinion leaders, source of interns, research supplier
Merchants	Potential customers
Opinion leaders	Source of opinion, votes
Other influentials	Recommenders

Nonprofits and educational institutions frequently take this approach, and it has the added benefit of helping to reduce your research costs. Remember, however, to do your best to compare apples to apples; for the University of New Hampshire, another state school in a small town would probably be an appropriate benchmark, but a private school in a large urban center would not.

Step 4: Set Your Audience Priorities: Who and What Is Most Important to Measure?

Now prioritize your audiences or stakeholder groups, which may be types of influencers (see Figure 9.1), other organizations, or even e-mail lists. Assume you will be able, at least at first, to measure at most three to five of these groups and that the audiences that are the most important get the greatest priority for measurement. For each audience, determine at least one measure of a successful relationship. It could be as simple as the number of desirable vs. undesirable stories about your organization that show up in the local paper, or the degree to which you are perceived to be the employer of choice in the area, or the increase in qualified applicants for jobs or volunteer positions.

Get everyone in your organization who will be impacted by the results of your measures to participate in the audience priority-setting. I give everyone a row of sticky dots (the kind you use for putting prices on items at garage sales) and tell everyone that each dot represents $1 million worth of budget to spend to influence the group. Each person can spend the dots however he or she sees fit. The audience with the greatest number of dots is the one you will measure first.

Step 5: Choose Your Measurement Tools

Once you've decided what other organizations or communities you are benchmarking against, you select your measurement tools.

Relationship Surveys   In general, the Grunig Relationship Survey, conducted online or by mail, is going to be your key source of data (see Chapter 4 and Appendix 1). Start with a benchmark survey to establish the existing level of trust and satisfaction with your stakeholders. As with any relationship study, you don't need to use all 75 Grunig statements to get a read on the community's pulse. A few in each category, focusing in particular on satisfaction and communal statements, will get you the data you need. Make sure you have a sufficiently large universe of respondents to enable you to segment the data by gender, geography, education, and length of time in the community.

Use questions like the following to measure audiences' sense of control mutuality.

- In dealing with people like me, this organization has a tendency to throw its weight around.
- This organization really listens to what people like me have to say.
- The management of this organization gives people like me enough say in the decision-making process.
- When I have an opportunity to interact with this organization, I feel that I have some sense of control over the situation.
- This organization won't cooperate with people like me.
- I believe people like me have influence on the decision makers of these organizations.

Use questions like these to measure trust and integrity:

- This organization treats people like me fairly and justly.
- Whenever this organization makes an important decision, I know it will be concerned about people like me.
- This organization can be relied on to keep its promises.
- I believe that this organization takes the opinions of people like me into account when making decisions.
- Sound principles seem to guide this organization's behavior.
- This organization does not mislead people like me.
- I am very willing to let this organization make decisions for people like me.
- I think it is important to watch this organization closely so that it does not take advantage of people like me.
- This organization is known to be successful at the things it tries to do.

Use questions like these to measure satisfaction:

- Both the organization and people like me benefit from the relationship.
- Most people like me are happy in their interactions with this organization.
- Generally speaking, I am pleased with the relationship this organization has established with people like me.
- Most people enjoy dealing with this organization.
- The organization fails to satisfy the needs of people like me.
- I feel people like me are important to this organization.
- In general, I believe that nothing of value has been accomplished between this organization and people like me.

Local Media Analysis Is Critical   Another way to test the health of relationships is to listen in on local conversations. Your local paper will have blogs and comment sections that will attract a wide range of opinions. Make sure you scan them on a regular basis to see if your organization is becoming the topic of a rumor or speculation. This will also alert you to potential outside influencers that may try to leverage a local crisis for their national agenda.

If your key source of influence is the local media, you will want to monitor it with media content analysis. This involves collecting items and mentions from all the local news outlets: TV, radio, online, weekly papers, dailies, blogs, Twitter feeds and Facebook pages, and if possible, any Listservs, community e-mail newsletters, or blogs. (For a more detailed discussion of media content analysis, see Chapter 4.) Make sure you are a subscriber to every source of news in the area, or, if you've hired a clipping agency, make sure it is tracking them all for you.

The importance of local e-mail lists and online publications cannot be overemphasized. The ease with which they pass along articles, news stories, and opinions can be a key factor in rallying supporters and protestors. Here in Durham, what started out years ago as a small meeting of friends became a 2,000-person politics-oriented mailing list that has elected conservation-oriented candidates, stopped the construction of a major sports complex (see the example in Chapter 14), blocked a number of housing developments, and become one of the biggest local sources of influential opinion.

A note about engagement: It's one thing to do CSR and community outreach as a way to mitigate a crisis or a problem. But more and more organizations are using these strategies to build engagement with their brand. Measuring engagement necessitates following the actions and desires of the customer. It doesn't matter what media your customers consume, it matters what they do with the information once they've gotten it. See Chapter 5 for detailed information about engagement and how to measure it.

Step 6: Analyze the Data

The next step is to analyze the media content to determine whether or not your community messages are being communicated. Find residents from your local community to read and code the articles or items, because only they will respond to them as your target audience(s) would.

Each article or item should be analyzed to determine to what extent the coverage is accurate, balanced, and fair. Are you getting more than your fair share of bad news? (That's why you want a peer organization to compare results with.) Track the source of each article or item: Was it generated by your department or by someone else in the local community? Who was quoted in the article or item, and did that quote reflect your desired positioning or messages? How visible are you?

Unlike in product PR, visibility at a local level is not necessarily desirable. It can make you a bigger target for protestors and for charitable organizations looking for corporate sponsors. I also recommend that you ask your readers to note how your organization is positioned in each article or item. Are you portrayed as an employer of choice or neighbor of choice? Are you described as concerned about the environment or the community?

When It Comes Up for a Vote, It's Too Late to Change Anything
If your objective is to create an environment in which expansion of your facility is welcome, the outcome of a critical vote is not a good measurement tool. Yes, a vote is an outcome, but once a motion comes before the town council or a local board, it is much too late to change anything. It can take 18 months to change people's minds on an issue, so don't wait until the month before a vote to launch your PR effort. Months before the vote is taken you need to understand how officials and townspeople perceive your organization, how they feel about the issues, and where they stand. If possible, poll them regularly, once a month or once a quarter, to see how opinions fluctuate.

Fishing in the Talent Pool?   If your objective is to be the employer of choice within the commutable area, keep tabs on requests for applications and responses to local ads. But just counting applications may not be enough. At least once a year you should survey the local community to find out how your organization is perceived as an employer. Again, use the Grunig instrument as discussed in Chapter 4 and Appendix 1.

Nonprofit Measures   If you are a nonprofit organization, size of donations and numbers of volunteers are clearly logical measures of success. However, the dollar amount of donations isn't an adequate measure, since many people will start with small donations and grow their commitment to your organization over time. A better measure is what percentage of the local community is donating. If possible, compare that share of wallet to other nonprofits in the area.

You must measure these outcomes on a regular basis—weekly or at least monthly. They are such important indicators that if they begin to decline you need to know immediately and you need to determine why. When revenues fall, organizations too frequently blame the economy or some outside force without any facts to back up the assertion. Regular relationship surveys of your community can provide the information you need to determine not just why revenues are down, but how you can improve them.

Government Can Plan—and Poll—Ahead   If you are a government institution, bottom-line measures like revenues, donations, or applications may not apply. What most government institutions want from their local communities is cooperation, trust, and support at the polls. Again, if you wait until election day to measure results, it will be too late to influence the outcome. Polling the community on a regular basis—ideally quarterly or at the very least every six months—will help you gauge sentiment and influence it in time to make a difference.

Campus Opportunities   If you have a college or university in your community, you may find some assistance with your research. Academic institutions have an advantage that many other organizations don't have—a genetic willingness to share information. Plus, they provide a built-in cadre of surveyors, researchers, and interns. If you are studying the local reputation of a college or university, chances are you can collaborate with other institutions to share costs.

CHAPTER 10

MEASURING WHAT YOUR EMPLOYEES THINK

"Research serves to make building stones out of stumbling blocks."
—Arthur D. Little

Given that employee morale and sentiment are closely tied to sales and profit, every business needs to continuously evaluate how employees perceive the organization. Do they recommend the business to friends as a great place to work? That lowers your recruitment costs. Do they buy or recommend the company's products? That means they'll advocate for your products in person and online. Do they believe your organization and management is honestly committed to its mission? That means they're more dedicated and productive.

IF EMPLOYEES ARE SO CONNECTED, WHY IS IT SO HARD TO COMMUNICATE WITH THEM?

In days gone by, when nets were something our grandmothers wore to control their hair and webs were where spiders hung out, companies had the mistaken notion that employees lived in glass bubbles. These employees obviously spoke a different language from anyone else on the planet; employee newsletters, videos, and internal communications departments all proved that. Somehow these workers were magically isolated from all other news sources

149

and therefore could be spoon-fed only the news chosen by their employers.

In fact, many companies thought that *all* their publics lived in isolated bubbles: investors, the media, overseas markets, distributors, and salespeople, and therefore, to communicate with each of these isolated publics, they had different silos. Because of this, each individual department tried to communicate with these separate audiences using different tools and different messages.

Social media has changed all that. Today, employees are more likely to get information about developments in your organization from blogs, text messaging, wikis, and e-mail. Media and information saturate our lives; with a few keystrokes, everyone has access to exactly the same information. So companies are responding and restructuring. The typical corporate communications manager I worked with 10 years ago now has responsibility for internal communications, investor relations, the company website, and international communications—in short, all of a company's possible constituencies. Increasingly, the employee communications function is moving out of the human resources department and into communications. If the responsibility stays in HR, a professional communicator from corporate communications staffs it. Such staffing makes perfect sense because top management understands the value of corporate communications to the bottom line.

Here's the reason: By providing information to employees about benefits, job openings, promotions, performance, productivity, organization events, and company goals and strategy, HR communications are a significant help to the functioning of the organization. But top management and smart managers recognize that a more strategically focused two-way dialogue with employees—one centered on meeting the organization's objectives—can have a direct and positive effect on the bottom line. For this reason companies need a skilled professional at the head of employee communications—one with a full understanding of organization direction, policy and procedure, structure, and goals.

On the other hand, it's harder than ever to reach employees and get them engaged with your organization's mission. They are already inundated with messages. Picture a typical employee who wakes up in the morning to NPR or talk radio, checks her Facebook and Twitter feeds, reads a few blogs and online news sources, reads the local paper, talks to friends in the car pool, talks to coworkers around the water cooler, and reads a number of magazines and blogs related to her job. After work, she sees ads at the grocery store and on the bus, talks to other parents at the children's football game, watches the evening news, catches a rerun of *The Daily Show* on Hulu, helps her child do her online homework, plays games on the Internet, checks out some of her favorite sites, and reads a mommy blog or two. Finally, having been bombarded with some 63,000 advertising messages along with countless other bits and bytes of information, she sinks into a well-deserved slumber.

Somehow, amidst all that clutter, the boss is trying to communicate some gobbledygook about mission, vision, or values, or yet another option in a benefits plan. The chances of the message getting through to the employee are only slightly better than the chances of getting hit by a meteor.

SEVEN STEPS TO MEASURING WHAT EMPLOYEES THINK, SAY, AND DO AS A RESULT OF YOUR INTERNAL COMMUNICATIONS

So how do you know if you've broken through all that clutter? Forget whether employees like the internal newsletter. What you need to find out first is which messages are getting through, how they're coming across, and through what media. Are they impacting the employees' loyalty, productivity, accuracy, or efficiency?

A simple measurement program will provide this information, but it takes a corporate-wide commitment to implement. Internal measurement projects sometimes don't happen—or have their results ignored—because they get caught up in internal politics, maybe as a perceived threat to a fiefdom or as a casualty of an internal war between department heads. To successfully measure your organization's relationship with its employees you must take these corporate politics into account and design your program to avoid pitfalls.

So here are the seven steps necessary to get an internal communications measurement program in place.

Step 1: Understand the Environment and Where They Really Get Information

A thorough, honest, and independent evaluation of existing communications—both official and unofficial sources of news and information—begins the process. Conduct a benchmark audit using the appropriate tools from the tools section below, or use data that is already available somewhere in the organization. This initial benchmark study may be more or less involved depending on the size and complexity of the organization, on what measurement tools are already being used, and on what data is already available.

First you need to collect and analyze samples of all the various news bites, rumors, and pieces of electronic as well as nonelectronic documentation that regularly bombard your employees.

How Are Messages Getting through to Employees, and What Are They? You've probably wondered more than once whether all those memos and e-mails are being read. Are they getting to people and/or departments in a timely manner? Are they being passed along or automatically deleted? Are they reaching the right people?

We refer to this phase of measurement as internal message analysis. We typically analyze all outgoing communications, including e-mails, newsletters, memos, voice mails, videos, speeches, and presentations to determine what messages are being communicated, who is getting the messages, and what they are doing with them, such as deleting them, forwarding them, or saving them for later. More sophisticated clients actually analyze the e-mail traffic to determine connections and networks that are developing. For large organizations, there are systems like Valdis Kreb's InFlow (www.orgnet.com/inflow3.html) to map the forwarding and response patterns of e-mail.

While most organizations are naturally concerned about over-surveying employees, a quick survey on e-mail usage generally pays off. JPMorgan Chase analyzed e-mail usage and discovered that by managing e-mail communications more efficiently, the organization could save several million dollars a year. Other important metrics are available from your intranet log files: What pages are people clicking on? What files are they downloading?

What Channels or Vehicles Do Employees Trust?   Of course we'd like employees to learn everything from official sources, but that just isn't going to happen. So you need to use your research to find out the influence of individual sources of information. Chat around the water cooler or coffeepot is probably a valuable source for some news, but as more and more workers telecommute there are fewer and fewer opportunities for that kind of casual communication. Instead, employees instant message or Skype or use Twitter to reach their colleagues. You will probably find that the company newsletter and company e-mail is important for other types of information.

Use either a formal survey or a focus group to find out what channels employees trust. Generally, employees find peers and immediate supervisors to be the most trustworthy, but this depends very much on the nature of the employee. One study we did revealed that engineers in a telecommunications company only trusted information they received electronically and inherently distrusted information delivered in big corporate meetings.

Note that child development researchers have discovered that different children learn in different ways. Some respond more readily to shapes and colors, others learn verbally from words and pictures, while still others learn aurally. To get all the children in a classroom to learn the same thing at the same time requires a cornucopia of teaching tools. The same is true for employee communications.

Caterpillar Inc., the tractor company, learned this lesson with regard to its internal communications program. The organization was accustomed to communicating internally in half a dozen different ways but found that it could never quite reach everyone all the time; some group of employees always remained uninformed. Consequently, Caterpillar decided to put out the same news in every format, and has found dramatic increases in employee knowledge of corporate messages. Different employees prefer different media for different types of news.

What's Important to Them?   Some 40 years ago, in a keynote address to the Advertising Club of St. Louis, Ralph Delahaye Paine (yes, a relative, my father, in fact), the editor of *Fortune*, mused, "If we can put a man in orbit, why can't we determine the effectiveness of our communications? The reason is simple and perhaps, therefore, a little old-fashioned: People, human beings with a wide range of choice. Unpredictable, cantankerous, capricious, motivated by innumerable conflicting interests and conflicting desires."

In the ensuing years, we have developed increasingly effective methods to measure people's capriciousness, but the reality remains that humans still hear what they want to hear. What they want to hear is what's important to them, perhaps what speaks to their most pressing and unfulfilled desires. If I need a new refrigerator because my old one is broken, I will be particularly receptive to news about refrigerators and ads for appliances. The same goes for your employees. If their biggest concerns revolve around the health of the organization and job security, then your messages about vision, values, and health care benefits will hardly register with them. If a number of pregnancies exist in a particular department, then benefits messages related to maternity leave and dependent insurance coverage will be picked up on first—you can bet on it.

What Do They Think about the Organization Today?   Existing perceptions play an enormous role in whether employees will receive whatever messages you're trying to communicate. If you don't know the health and strength of your relationship with them, you have no idea whether they're likely to listen to what you have to say. And then, given the nature of the relationship, you still need to get them to tell you if they understand the vision and values: Do they have an understanding of what the organization is trying to do?

In some companies we find that the space between line workers and management opens to such an extent that internal communicators need to start by educating employees about what business the organization is in. Other companies are at the opposite end of the scale, using open-book management to keep every employee informed of not just the organization's business but the actual financial details of the operation as well.

Step 2: Agree on Clear, Measurable Goals

Now that you thoroughly understand the environment and your starting point, it is time to get agreement from top management about what you're trying to accomplish. To do this you need to understand the vision, objectives, and messages that senior management wants to communicate and what they expect of HR and your communications effort.

First, you will probably want to present to key management the information from your benchmark studies in Step 1 so that they understand the context. Even if, for timing or other reasons, a formal presentation may not be practical, you or your research partner will want to interview key management and determine what their messages and objectives are. Based on a thorough analysis of your preparatory research, write down very clear, explicit objectives and get senior management to agree to them. What do they think is important? What do they see as the corporate vision? What do they see as the strategic direction? Is the goal of your internal communications program to increase loyalty and productivity? To decrease employee turnover? To help in recruitment efforts? Is the goal to communicate specific messages?

Remember that what you measure is dependent upon the goals of your communications efforts. If you are using Twitter for recruitment, for example, getting more followers is not the goal. Finding better qualified, more engaged employees is the desired result. So you need to have systems in place to track not just the quantity of applications but the quality as well. You'll probably want to know if using Twitter has resulted in lower recruitment costs and less employee turnover.

If your goal is greater engagement in the company's mission, you need to determine how engaged employees are today, and then set reasonable goals for how much more engaged you think they should be after your strategy is in place. So a good goal might be: Get 50 percent of all employees engaged by a particular date. You then need to get consensus on specifically what it means to be engaged and how you are going to measure it. Does that mean heavier use of the Intranet as measured by web stats? More knowledge and buy-in with the mission as measured by a survey? Each has different metrics and requires different measurement tools.

Step 3: Select a Benchmark to Compare To

Measurement is a comparative tool, and you have to decide what you want to be compared to. It would be nice to be able to compare your results to robust industry-wide statistics, but internal communications measurement is such a young field that few are available. Watson Wyatt Worldwide does a number of studies of corporate communications that provide general benchmark data such as: Companies that communicate effectively are 4.5 times more likely to report high employee engagement and 20 percent more likely to report lower turnover rates when compared to firms that communicate less effectively. A recent study found that firms within the financial and wholesale/retail trade sectors rank among the most effective communicators, while companies from the basic materials, general services, and health care sectors tend to rank among the least effective communicators. (http://www.towerswatson.com/research/670.)

Most organizations compare results only year to year, but we strongly recommend more frequently, at least twice a year. Another recommended approach is to find a peer organization. The comparison doesn't even have to be with an organization in your industry. Telecommunications companies have been known to benchmark against Disney and General Electric because the latter had similar programs.

The bottom line is that you need to benchmark your results to an entity that seems credible to your boss or your board. If you are a telecommunications organization and your boss admires Disney, compare yourself to Disney. You and your results will get more respect than if you compare yourself to an organization that the boss does not respect.

Step 4 : Define the Criteria of Success

This is where you decide what truly defines your success, and where you commit to achieving specific goals. Make sure your goals are achievable. This process involves defining the actual words and numbers to be used as you create your specific, measurable definitions of success. These criteria are numerical, and most often they are percentages or amounts expressed in dollars or numbers of something. Your definition(s) of success might include, for instance:

- My program will increase understanding of the corporate mission and values by X percent.
- My program will decrease employee turnover by X percent.

Step 5: Select Your Measurement Tools and Collect Data

The tools that will provide the data and statistics you use to evaluate and compare programs are surveys, media content and message analysis, and web analytics. The specific tools we recommend are discussed below. They're all widely available, and many may already be in place within your organization.

Message Analysis Tools   Internal communications never functions in a vacuum. Employees are just as likely to get news of company developments from the local media or the gossip at a soccer game as they are from your e-mails. Therefore, it is critical that you monitor local media (especially blogs) to have a complete understanding of what the employee is seeing. For more on media content analysis, refer to Chapter 4.

You will also want to conduct a survey that will help you determine what the takeaways are from the messages you are trying to communicate. In other words, did employees understand the message; did they interpret it correctly? Did it change their morale, their work habits, or their level of understanding? To what extent did your communications affect their outlook toward the company? We recommend quarterly pulse checks of employee attitudes to determine how perceptions are changing over time.

Focus groups can help you discover the real issues that concern employees and the specifics you want to measure. If the major messages aren't getting through, what is? What are the subtle variations between what the head honchos say and what the employees hear?

Outcome Measurement Tools   Outcomes are the behaviors that you want to effect within your organization. Ideally, your communications efforts are intended to make employees more knowledgeable, more loyal, more efficient, and more productive. So your outcome metrics might be employee retention, performance ratings, turnover, or efficiency ratings.

One company developed an ongoing Trivial Pursuit-type quiz to test employees' knowledge and understanding of their messages. Prizes were awarded for the most right answers. The program significantly increased employee's understanding and belief in the company's key messages.

An important outcome metric is available by studying your intranet's log files. Data such as how long employees spend in each area, what pages they visit, and the extent to which they download the information you provide are all potentially valuable measures of employee behavior.

Increasingly, organizations are using internal blogs and communities as a way to get messages out to employees and to gather feedback from employees. Companies like Sun and GM rely on blogs to establish two-way conversations between management and employees. If you have a corporate blog you have an easy way to track employee responses based not just on the direct comments, but also on the volume of traffic, the number of trackbacks, and the number of other links to the site.

Use Surveys to Determine What Employees Think   For surveys to be statistically valid, every employee needs an equal opportunity to participate. In many companies this precludes e-mail surveys, since not every employee has equal access to computers. In many cases even phones aren't always within reach. No surprise, then, that so many companies still rely on paper surveys. Although they may be slow and appear antiquated, employees seem remarkably willing to fill them out. A good response rate for employee paper surveys is around 40 percent.

Phone surveys are a good option for those groups of employees, like managers, for instance, who definitely have phones. We undertook a survey for a major national health concern and found that more than half of the survey population willingly spent 30 minutes with us, discussing the pros and cons of the communications program.

The key, of course, is to ask the right questions. Make sure that you have a professional researcher craft the survey questionnaire and include demographics by which you can segment the data. Look around any company Christmas party and you'll quickly realize that

employees are hardly a single audience. You'll see long-time employees and newbies, men and women, geeks and marketers, telecom-
muters and cubicle dwellers, branch office and main office. So don't
measure them as if they're one group.

Designing a survey is a deceptively difficult job, and if you get it
wrong, you probably won't find out until there's a pile of worthless
paper staring you in the face. We often see homegrown benchmarking programs fail because the right questions either were not asked or
were asked in a way that failed to yield actionable information. Too
many employee attitude surveys measure tactics rather than relationships. The right way to measure employee attitude is not just to test
satisfaction but to use the Grunig Relationship Survey questions (see
Chapter 4 and Appendix 1).

Step 6 : Analyze and Take Action

After you have collected the data, it needs to be counted, evaluated,
and categorized according to type, effectiveness, messages communicated, and so forth. Examine what messages are being delivered in
what formats. You can use something as simple as an Excel spreadsheet, or a more sophisticated database package like WinCross, SAS,
or SPSS to dig a little deeper.

Make sure you analyze your data by segment. At the very least you
will want to compare data by: gender, age, length of time with the
company, title/level, exempt vs. nonexempt, and geographic location.

Many organizations standardize on cost-per-message-communi-
cated as a way to compare the efficiency and effectiveness of different programs. This requires taking your employee communications
budget and dividing it by the number of messages communicated.
Another option is to compare the reach and frequency of message
communications in various different vehicles, including e-mail, local
media, and internal communiqués. You'll probably want to compare
and contrast internal versus external communications vehicles to test

the degree to which different media outlets and different tactics are successful in communicating your messages.

The point of measurement is not simply to generate a folder full of charts and graphs. You want to glean insight, draw conclusions, and make recommendations. The idea is to use your hard-won knowledge to improve the effectiveness of what you are doing. Therefore, you want to have results in hand when decisions can be made and steps taken toward improvement.

Set up a regular schedule for reporting and planning. "Last week" is generally when most companies need the results of their bench-marking studies. Realistically, you need to work backward from when the results will do the most good. If you do your planning in July and get results in January, the results are six months too late and you're dealing with very old news. You don't want a message *du jour*, but you do want to engender consistency and continuity, so we recommend benchmarking every 12 to 18 months.

Make Changes to Improve Employee Relationships

One important rule of employee communications is that once you have conducted a survey, employees will expect change to happen. The very act of surveying raises expectations that things will improve or at least change. Getting back to employees after you do the research is especially important, not just with results but with specific changes that you will make or recommend.

So whatever you do, don't keep the data to yourself. Post it on an internal blog or intranet site for everyone to see. While your experts can do the formal analysis, don't be afraid to solicit input, comments, and interpretations from all of your employees. You may want to conduct additional focus groups to explain or interpret data that seems perplexing. As soon as possible, communicate any changes that will be occurring as a result of your research. That way, you ensure participation in future research.

CHAPTER 11

THREATS TO YOUR REPUTATION: HOW TO MEASURE CRISES

"Far more crucial than what we know or do not know is what we do not want to know. One often obtains a clue to a person's nature by discovering the reasons for his or her imperviousness to certain impressions."

—Eric Hoffer

Your reputation is the sum total of your relationships with all your publics. It is what people think of when they hear your brand mentioned; it determines the likelihood that they purchase or recommend your products, invest in your company, or apply for a job. It also influences the likelihood that your opponents will sue you, protest at your doorstep, or write letters to government officials complaining about you. Trust between your organization and your publics is the foundation of your reputation. To paraphrase Arthur Page, in a democratic society, any organization continues to exist only because society gives it permission to. And the giving or withholding of that permission is based largely on your reputation.

Assuming you've been around for a while, your reputation already exists in the minds of your stakeholders. It is not something that will change overnight, because relationships don't change overnight.

Trust, commitment, and satisfaction take a long time to build up, but they can all be destroyed in seconds.

Crises occur when events threaten your reputation. The key to measuring threats to your reputation is measuring the trust between you and your publics, and the effectiveness with which your organization handles crises.

Of course, the best type of crisis communications is that which avoids the crisis altogether. In fact, according to James Grunig, good crisis communications starts long before an incident occurs:

> Communication with publics before decisions are made is most effective in resolving issues and crises because it helps managers to make decisions that are less likely to produce consequences that publics make into issues and crises. If public relations staff does not communicate with its publics until an issue or crisis occurs, the chance of resolving the conflict is slim.
> —Grunig, Grunig, and Dozier, 2002

Grunig, Grunig, and Dozier articulate four principles of crisis a period, like: communications.

- *The Relationship Principle:* An organization can withstand both issues and crises better if it has established good, long-term relationships with publics who are at risk from decisions and behaviors of the organization.
- *The Accountability Principle:* An organization should accept responsibility for a crisis even if it was not its fault.
- *The Disclosure Principle:* At the time of a crisis, an organization must disclose all that it knows about the crisis or problem involved. If it does not know what happened, then it must promise full disclosure once it has additional information.
- *The Symmetrical Communication Principle:* At the time of a crisis, an organization must consider the public interest to be at least as important as its own. Public safety, for example, is at least as important as profits. Therefore, the organization has no choice other than to engage in true dialogue with publics and to practice socially responsible behavior when a crisis occurs.

To simplify: The single best way to avoid a crisis is to listen carefully to your audiences and respond to threats *before* they get out of hand. Remember that it only takes an hour or so for a YouTube video to be seen by tens of thousands of people and for a TV crew to show up on your doorstep. So daily monitoring via Google Alerts or Social Mention is an absolute necessity these days. Determine not just what they are saying about you, but more important, what issues are surfacing in Twitter or newsgroups, as well as the media. How are employees, vendors, and the community responding to your messages? These questions can easily be answered through regular surveys and media content analysis.

But sometimes all the listening in the world cannot prevent the unavoidable accident or the simple twist of fate. Through no fault of your own an angry customer tweets about his or her experience, others chime in, and soon there's a full-fledged Twitstorm flying around your brand. The next day the TV cameras show up and the spotlight is on you. If you're prepared, then your crisis communications plan kicks into effect, your key messages are delivered, and the emergency website goes live. And if you're not prepared, then you'll be misquoted, appear to be out of control, and the crisis will deepen.

So, assuming that your organization has followed all the rules, how do you know how well you're doing under fire? The answer is that you measure three variables: What is being *said* about you, what people *believe* about you, and what people *do* as a result.

MEASURING WHAT IS BEING SAID ABOUT YOU

Your media monitoring report should typically cover print, television, radio, online news sources, blogs, Facebook threads, tweets, YouTube videos, Flickr sets, social bookmarks, bulletin boards, forums, communities, and any other source of information that exists in your marketplace. Let me be perfectly clear, monitoring mainstream media is not enough. You need to listen to what your customers are saying.

As an example, look at the infamous Dell Hell crisis. For years people had been complaining in blogs and to friends about how awful Dell's customer service was. In fact, I myself always refused to purchase a Dell computer because time and again I'd hear my employees spending hours on the phone with tech support trying to solve simple problems. Eventually a prominent blogger wrote about a problem he had and thousands of angry customers chimed in with similar horror stories. Even so, this might not have had a huge impact on Dell, except that the story crossed from social media to mainstream media and the company's stock price took a dive. It took Dell many years of listening to customers, apologizing, and fixing their computers to restore the company's image. And it took lots of deep discounts to get people to buy products that had a poor reputation for reliability. So the implications of a crisis aren't just unquantifiable, squishy touchy-feely things, they have a direct impact on your bottom-line profitability and stock price.

How you listen to your customers and measure trust can have a major impact on your organization. Later we'll go into the specific steps you'll need to follow to establish a methodology and data management program, but the point is that you absolutely need to have a system in place to analyze what is being said, how the organization is being positioned, and what messages are being delivered. Let's face it, when a crisis hits, adrenalin-fueled gut feelings are not the most reliable decision-making tools. So you need data that comes from daily—or even hourly—monitoring of what is being said about you. Schedule delivery of these reports to allow plenty of time to craft and refine the key messages you need to be communicating. Ideally, your monitoring would also include qualitative analysis to determine the major issues and sentiments being expressed.

Sometimes the ultimate measure isn't the content but the sheer volume of crisis coverage. The charts in Figures 11.1 and 11.2 track the volume of mentions over time for several well-known crises. As you can see, sometimes the volume of coverage goes up after the crisis breaks and sometimes it goes down. That's the difference between

Figure 11.1
Volume of coverage over time for three crises.

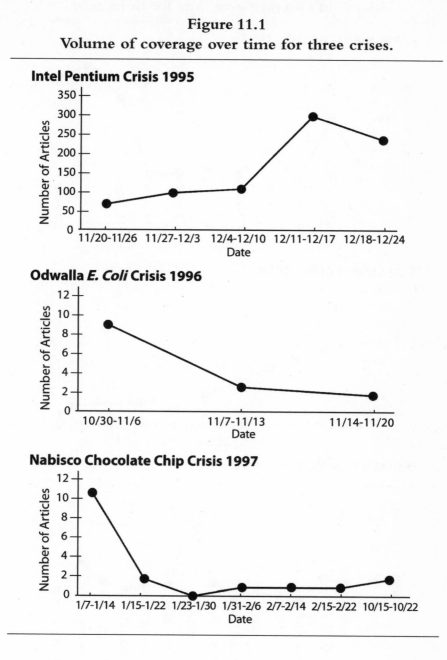

Figure 11.2
Volume of coverage over time for three crises.

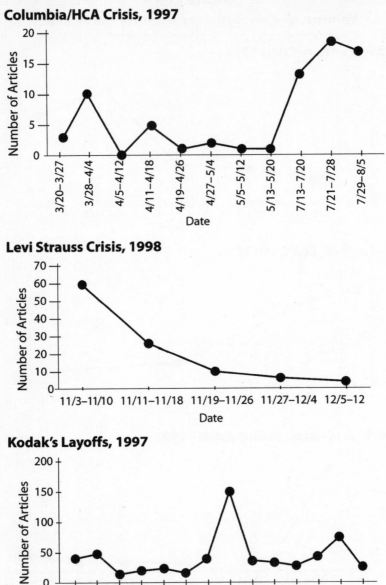

Columbia/HCA Crisis, 1997

Levi Strauss Crisis, 1998

Kodak's Layoffs, 1997

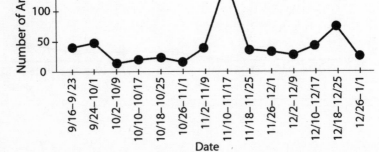

well-managed crises and poorly handled ones. A well-managed crisis gets all the bad news over with up front by aggressively dealing with the problem, and the volume drops precipitously after the first week. The fallout from a poorly handled crisis can drag on for months.

Odwalla, a natural juice company, was found to have sold batches of contaminated, unpasteurized apple juice that sickened a number of people and resulted in the death of a child. Its corporate culture, reputation for social responsibility, and crisis communications were so strong, however, that it managed to contain the crisis in a few short weeks and ultimately avoided lawsuits altogether.

While Nabisco's story isn't as dramatic, it demonstrates how fast thinking on the part of a member of the public relations team saved the day. An elementary school class released a story saying that Nabisco's Chips Ahoy chocolate chip cookies did not, in fact, have as many chips per bag as promised. The company immediately sent a "cookie technician" to the school in North Carolina to help the class repeat the experiment. The new study found more chips than promised and the crisis coverage was gone within a week.

Not so the case of Columbia/HCA Healthcare, which denied and obfuscated its financial results for so long that the story dragged on for months and eventually lead to the replacement of all top management.

In the case of Levi Strauss's first-ever layoffs, the company took a novel proactive approach by simultaneously announcing grants to all the communities affected. As a result, its coverage spiked the first week and steadily decreased after that.

Unlike Levi Strauss, Kodak Corporation suffered a series of leaks about potential layoffs, eventually announced layoffs, and then had to announce even more layoffs, because the cuts hadn't been deep enough. Again, the result was many, many weeks of bad news.

MEASURING WHAT PEOPLE BELIEVE ABOUT YOU

Looking at the volume of clips after the fact is one way to judge how effective your actions were, but just getting the messages out into the world is seldom enough to turn around a crisis. Frequently you need to ensure that those messages are being heard and believed as they are going out. The best way to check in with your key audiences in a crisis is through overnight polling. One cost-effective way to conduct overnight polling is to add a question to an omnibus poll. Alternatively, you can commission your own overnight telephone poll, which can cost anywhere from $5,000 to $25,000. Yes, it's expensive. But, given the cost of talking to your audiences with a full-page ad in the *New York Times* ($100,000), the cost of listening with an overnight poll seems comparatively cheap. And compared to the legal, personnel, and emotional costs of a protracted crisis, research always represents a relatively small percentage of expenditures.

For example, a prominent high-tech company had been a major Olympic sponsor for several years, providing a large scale computer installation for the Games. The week before the Games were to open it was discovered that parts of the system didn't work, specifically in the media center. The media went ballistic and published story after story detailing the failings of the system. However, in overnight polling, the company was able to determine that its core customer base wasn't negatively affected by the coverage, but was in fact highly supportive. Despite the ongoing media outcry, the poll data served to calm executives and enabled the company to make rational decisions to deal with the crisis.

TRUST IS THE KEY TO BUILDING AND DEFENDING YOUR REPUTATION

Trust, or lack thereof, has a measurable effect on the financial health of any organization because it affects customer loyalty, word of mouth, employee retention, and ultimately, reputation. In fact, the foundation of your reputation is the trust that exists between your organization and your publics. The biggest damage a badly managed crisis will have on your organization is what it does to that trust, and to the relationships and reputation built on it. As we shall see, trust between individuals and organizations has been widely studied. Measuring it is a vital component to both building your reputation and defending against crises.

You need look no further than the accounting firm Arthur Andersen to see evidence that lack of trust can ruin a company. Arthur Anderson was destroyed after the Enron scandal not because of financial wrongdoing, but because its clients lost their trust in its results. Likewise, in the world of fast food, whenever news of tainted beef hits the airwaves, consumers lose trust in the safety of their favorite burger and McDonald's sales take a dive. Conversely, a key to FedEx's success is that customers *do* trust the company's pledge to deliver "when it absolutely, positively has to be there" overnight.

Thanks to the economic collapse of 2008, people trust corporations less than at almost any other time in our history. Thus, when trust helps an organization build relationships with key constituencies, it saves that organization money by reducing the costs of litigation, regulation, legislation, pressure campaigns, boycotts, and lost revenue.

- A high level of trust helps cultivate relationships with donors, consumers, investors, and legislators who are needed to support organizational goals.
- When employees trust their employer they are more likely to support the mission of the organization and be satisfied with their jobs.
- Lower employee turnover has a direct impact on the bottom line.
- Trust from the financial community is critical to an organization's access to capital and, therefore, its ability to grow.
- Good relationships with the media can often avert a crisis.

The essential transparency of social media has also helped redefine the importance and relevance of trust in today's marketplace. If you are doing—or perceived to be doing—something wrong, bad, or hurtful, chances are that someone will report it somewhere in social media. If you're lucky it won't be filmed and end up on YouTube.

If your stakeholders have a high degree of trust in your organization it's likely they'll come to your defense, and what could have been a devastating scandal may be forgiven in a day or two.

Even though examples such as these make it clear that trust is important, few companies actually measure the trust that their constituencies have in them.

What Is Trust? Trust has been a widely studied concept both by itself and, most important, as a component of the quality of relationships. Research by Jim Grunig and Linda Hon has shown that trust is one of six independently measurable components of relationships. Jim Grunig has identified three dimensions of trust that are measurable by the Grunig Relationship Survey.

1. *Competence:* The belief that an organization has the ability to do what it says it will do, including the extent to which an organization is seen as being effective and that it can compete and survive in the marketplace.
2. *Integrity:* The belief that an organization is fair and just.
3. *Dependability/reliability:* The belief that an organization will do what it says it will do, that it acts consistently and dependably.

Although the experts are not in complete agreement, trust between an organization and its publics is generally described as having the following independently quantifiable characteristics:

- *Multilevel.* Trust results from interactions that span coworker, team, organizational, and interorganizational alliances. This is why you need to cast a wide net when you survey your publics on trust.
- *Culturally rooted.* Trust is closely tied to the norms, values, and beliefs of the organizational culture. Therefore, it is critical to understand the self-image and self-definitions of your publics if you are going to accurately measure trust.

- *Communication-based.* Trust is the outcome of communications behaviors, such as providing accurate information, giving explanations for decisions, and demonstrating sincere and appropriate openness. This is why communications metrics are critical in trust measurement.
- *Dynamic.* Trust is constantly changing as it cycles through phases of building, destabilization, and dissolving. So it is important to measure trust on a continuum over time.
- *Multidimensional.* Trust consists of multiple factors at the cognitive, emotional, and behavioral levels, all of which affect an individual's perceptions of trust.

Just to add another wrinkle to this discussion, Andrew Tucker, in a paper delivered at the 2006 International Public Relations Research Conference (IPRRC), postulated three measurable varieties of trust:

- *Short-term trust*, which is based on financial performance and product quality metrics like *Fortune's* Most Admired list.
- *Medium-term trust*, which translates roughly to, "I can't totally trust you because I don't know you, but I need to trust you somewhat to do my job or fill my need."
- *Long-term trust*, which is based on customer loyalty.

I believe that there's another variety of trust. "Reflexive trust" occurs when a source loses its trustworthiness because of frequent obfuscation or spin, and, as a result, an opposing or contradictory source takes on greater trustworthiness. You frequently see this in politics when people perceive the incumbent party to have lied or in some way been corrupt. People then seem to trust the opponents, even though they lack a proven track record.

The media provides another example. Today it seems that more and more people are choosing to consume media based on whether they believe the network or source. So no matter how much fact-based evidence there is on one side of the story, just because that side is saying it, people will believe the opposite. There's a lesson in this for many organizations: If you consistently obfuscate, lie, and spin, at some point your very statements begin to enhance your competitor's credibility.

BS Is More Damaging than Lies   That's exactly what Brad Rawlins and Kevin Stoker were talking about in their 2006 IPRRC paper on BS in PR. Their point was that bullshit is more damaging than lies. Liars, they argue, have a fundamental respect for—or at least knowledge of—the truth, and they choose not to use it. Bullshitters (and, I argue, those who spin PR), on the other hand, use language to blur the truth, and are intentionally careless and vague about the truth. Rawlins and Stoker cite *On Bullshit*, by Henry G. Frankfurt. Frankfurt's point is that bullshit isn't false, it's fake. Its intent is not to mislead about facts but about impressions and to create favorable impressions despite unfavorable facts.

Rawlins and Stoker argue that bullshit is insidious not because the person speaking the bullshit believes it, but because he is trying to manipulate people with it. That is the same argument many in social media make about corporate PR types trying to fake their way into the medium. Rawlins and Stoker suggest that we need to change this environment and inject more honesty, loyalty, and moral values into what we say and write as part of our profession. In this new era of transparency, your target audience is putting greater value on character. To increase your trustworthiness and credibility, take responsibility for your actions, and make sure that the things you do and the things you espouse and believe in are the same. Rawlins argues that this is not just a virtuous model but good corporate strategy.

Even more important, a business that attempts to obfuscate its statements reduces confidence not just in the organization but in the individuals at the top. The bottom line according to Rawlins: Hold on to the virtue. Abandon the vices. Get rid of the disconnect between what you believe and what you do. Work for organizations that exhibit character in the way they operate, in their visions, and values. If the organization doesn't have character and hasn't changed its character to correct a crisis, then you are communicating bullshit. "You have to be willing to say the things that no one wants to hear," said Rawlins. His final point—which returns to my point about reflexive trust—is that if everything we say is tainted by bullshit, no one will believe anything we try to communicate.

MEASURING WHAT PEOPLE DO: LONG-TERM EFFECTS AND FOLLOW-UP RESEARCH

While every crisis differs, follow-up research is critical. No matter what the nature of the crisis or the organization, the best thing that can come of a crisis is learning from your mistakes. Post-mortem measurement examines not just how well you did at getting messages communicated, but it also demonstrates what ultimate outcomes the crisis communication program had. Did consumers change their behavior? Did employees leave at a higher than normal rate? Did the stock drop? Did your trust level on Wall Street change? Did your relationships with your employees improve or deteriorate?

Some of these measures are easy, such as looking at the stock price and adjusting for other activity in the market as a whole. Tracking consumer behavior requires broader cooperation within the organization. Frequently, consumer data is readily available from your organization's market research department. There are also many firms that specialize in integrated marketing research. One such firm, Loyalty Builders (www.loyaltybuilders.com), examines customer transactions to determine the impact of events on customer loyalty. It examines how frequently customers purchase, the amount of their purchases, and the time between purchases. You can plot that data against your crisis data and look for possible connections.

Even if you don't have customers, you may still need to check on the ultimate impact of a crisis on your target audiences. That's what Habitat for Humanity did after a television reporter in Chicago launched an investigation of its Chicago office. Concerned that the negative publicity might discourage volunteers from participating or donors from giving to the program, it commissioned a survey of target audience members to determine what impact the publicity had on Habitat's reputation. The study showed that, thanks to a coordinated and consistent effort to provide facts, figures, and information—and thanks to the fact that the organization had such strong relationships with its constituencies to begin with—the negative publicity achieved scant awareness and had no influence on Habitat's audience.

Similar results were found in a research study for a waste disposal company in Texas. The company had sued a television station for libel, charging that a negative story about its dumping of sludge wastes had damaged its reputation. Follow-up survey research discovered that very few people remembered seeing the show and no one remembered the name of the company.

SEVEN STEPS TO MEASURE CRISES AND TRUST

Measurement of trust and your relationships during and after a crisis involves many of the same components of the seven steps that we discussed in Chapter 3.

It seeks to answer questions such as:

- Have the behaviors, programs, and activities we implemented changed what people know, think, and feel about the organization, and how they actually act (as exhibited by protests, votes, and purchases)?
- Have the actions or behaviors of our organization had an effect on the trust that our constituencies feel toward our organization?
- Have the public relations and communications efforts that were initiated to build trust had an effect? If so, how can we support and document that with research?

Work through the first steps below well before you see any crisis coming, because when it does hit, you won't have time to do any careful preparation; you'll be struggling just to keep pace with the events of the day.

Step 1: Define a Specific Desired Outcome from the Crisis

Most people would say that just surviving the crisis is goal enough. But you need to make sure that everyone agrees on what surviving looks like:

- Is a 10 percent decline in stock price acceptable? Or does that put the ownership of the company at risk, as happened to BP in the midst of the Gulf oil spill? Its stock price dropped so precipitously and for so long that it became vulnerable to a takeover bid.
- If you are a consumer company, is a 10 percent or 20 percent drop in sales acceptable in a recall situation, or does that jeopardize your market share and ability to attract talent?
- If you are a nonprofit and donations decline by 10 percent, is that acceptable or does that hurt cash flow enough to put the organization's viability at stake?

Plan ahead, consider various damage scenarios, and set a clear definition of what success in a crisis will mean to your company or organization.

If you already are in a crisis, your first step is to define your goals for the crisis at hand. Do you just want to minimize the negatives, do you want to avoid lawsuits, or do you want to do better than the competition?

Step 2: Define Your Audiences and What You Want Your Relationships to Be with Each One

If you haven't already, you need to identify those groups or individuals with whom your organization has or needs relationships. The first step is to gather in one room your top-tier managers from marketing, sales, employee communications, and anyone else in your organization who can help you define important crisis audiences. List all the possible audiences, including employees, customers, prospects, volunteers, attendees, donors, sponsors, investors or shareholders, the distribution channel, vendors and suppliers, the local constituency, and regulators.

Now define how a good relationship with each audience can help in a crisis and how a bad relationship can hurt in a crisis. It might be that a good relationship does nothing more than prevent lawsuits or it may be that it results in sales. Either way, you need to articulate what the specific benefits are of your efforts for each audience. Because, if in fact the relationship turns bad and the benefits go away, then you need to quantify the failure as well.

Prioritize the audiences and get senior management to agree to those priorities. This prioritization is important because it determines what channels, publications, and media outlets you monitor. For example, if major shareholders are your top priority, you'll want to be particularly concerned about what is being said and heard on Wall Street. However, if you are a small, nonpublic business faced with an environmental scandal just as plans for your plant expansion are going before the local planning board, tracking what is said in local papers and blogs or on the sidelines of the middle school soccer field might be considerably more important.

Step 3: Define Your Benchmark

In a crisis, an organization typically measures its own progress over time. It can be significantly more revealing, however, to measure a crisis against some other control group. For example, a study of an airline in crisis looked at its coverage in its hometown paper vs. coverage in five other cities. The study revealed that, in contrast to the assumptions of the CEO, the local paper actually covered the airline more favorably than did papers in other cities, because it tended to provide more in-depth stories, rather than just the negative financials. A similar study compared a company in crisis to other companies in the same town and revealed just how seriously negative the company's coverage actually was.

Step 4: Define Your Measurement Criteria

No one can really measure the effectiveness of anything without first figuring out exactly what it is they are measuring. So, how will you define success in this circumstance?

You may well have different goals for different stakeholder groups. List the benefits a good relationship with each segment or audience will deliver to the organization. You will use this list of benefits to create specific criteria against which you can measure your success. Criteria are the hard numbers, complete with a time frame. For example: "Communicate key messages in 40 percent of all articles over the next two months," or, "Keep negative messages during the crisis to no more than 10 percent of all coverage."

Today, timing is a key element in any crisis measurement program. While in the past, decisions and official statements may have waited until the deadline, with the advent of social media there is no deadline. The clock starts ticking from the first tweet, and people will pay very close attention to the timing of your reactions. In a famous kerfuffle between prominent blogger Robert Scoble and Facebook, the influential blogger Shel Israel commented on Twitter: "It's been three hours and no response yet from Facebook." Where you used to have hours, you now have minutes to articulate a response. So tracking reaction on an hourly basis is critical.

Typical Performance Indicators
- Percent increase in trust scores.
- Percent of coverage containing key messages.
- Share of desirable versus undesirable coverage.

Step 5: Select a Measurement Tool

There is no one, simple, all-encompassing research tool, technique, or methodology you can rely on to measure and evaluate relationships and trust during a crisis. You will usually need to devise a combination of different measurement techniques appropriate for your situation. Some of the tools and techniques to measure trust include:

- Surveys
- Focus groups
- Before-and-after polls
- Ethnographic studies
- Experimental and quasi-experimental designs
- Multivariate analysis projects
- Model building
- Content analysis

To measure the perceptions of an organization's relationships with key constituencies, we suggest administering a questionnaire that includes a series of agree/disagree statements pertaining to the relationship, such as those used in the Grunig Relationship Survey (see Chapter 4 and Appendix 1). Respondents are asked to use a scale of one to seven to indicate the extent to which they agree or disagree that each item listed describes their relationship with that particular organization.

Over the long term, the value of increasing the level of trust in your organization can be measured in money saved from lower costs of expansion, lower litigation fees, lower costs of recruitment and, ultimately, lower cost of operations.

The important point here is to plan ahead and budget accordingly. The general rule of thumb is to allocate 5 to 10 percent of your budget to measurement, but in a crisis, this percentage could be significantly larger, depending on the issues and the complexity of the situation. Remember, good measurement can help you shorten the duration of a crisis, and measurement is cheap compared to the cost of rebuilding your relationships and your reputation.

Step 6: Analyze Results, Glean Insight, and Make Actionable Recommendations

The most important part of the measurement process is to analyze the data and learn from it. What are the actionable points; how can you change and improve? What should you react to? What should you ignore? What needs to be done today?

The most valuable data from crisis measurement may be the list you will have developed of bloggers and other individuals who are now interested in your organization and will most likely write about you again in social media. You also need to evaluate the impact of any interaction you may have. Pay particular attention if you have a corporate spokesperson who has reached out to a blogger and has turned a potentially negative perspective neutral. First identify any opposition to management goals and decisions before it results in a crisis or develops into an issue with your constituencies. Second, use your data to help management understand that certain decisions might have adverse consequences on the public's trust.

There are many times when improved trust or relationships do not lead to immediate changes in behavior, so it is important to set realistic expectations. Trust and good relationships keep publics from engaging in negative behaviors such as litigation, strikes, protests, or unflattering publicity. It is very difficult to measure a behavior that did not occur because of a good relationship. If a controversy never hits the media as a result of relationship-building efforts, and if you are only measuring media relations, then you will have no data to show that your relationship-building efforts worked.

At other times, there may be a long lead time between the development of a good relationship and a behavior. For example, if you make a habit of inviting members of a community to social events and other relationship-building occasions, they may see you as friendlier or nicer or easier to deal with. As a result, you are more likely to find that differences or misunderstandings between that audience and your organization can be resolved by conversations rather than litigation. However, it may take months or, more likely, years before your social efforts have a measurable effect on legal fees.

One way around this is to interview members of the community to test their perceptions. Another way to approach it is to look at your organization's share of negatives as compared to that of peer companies or competitors. If your share of negatives is declining while the others are holding steady or going up, you know your strategy is working.

Step 7: Make Changes and Measure Again

Your data-driven insights and recommendations ensure that your measurement system is perceived as worthwhile. Don't be afraid to stand up for them during the crisis and afterward, as well. Your measurement program will become more respected and you'll be better at it if you continue the program after the crisis is over. Measurement should always be ongoing and an integral part of your organizational strategy.

CHAPTER 12

MEASURING RELATIONSHIPS WITH SALESPEOPLE, CHANNEL PARTNERS, AND FRANCHISEES

"The only man I know who behaves sensibly is my tailor; he takes my measurements anew each time he sees me. The rest go on with their old measurements and expect me to fit them."

—George Bernard Shaw

If management is from Mars (see the introduction to the Glossary) and the rest of us are from Venus, then salespeople are from a different solar system altogether. Whether they're your own internal sales force, franchisees, or channel partners, they are very distinctly "other," isolated either by geography, legal standing, or responsibility. Unlike PR people, who spend most of their waking hours worrying about the media or their internal clients, salespeople spend *all* their waking hours, and most of their sleeping ones as well, worrying about the customer.

Over the years, as my companies have developed several ways of measuring relationships with salespeople, we have had to take into account their very different perspective. First of all, you can anticipate their attitude to be: "I'm expected to spend my time selling, but the home office deluges me with new products and new information that

I'm supposed to find time to read and talk about with the clients. And then, of course, the really important stuff the home office never tells you about; you have to find that out from the local papers, the customers or, worse yet, the competition." Yes, we have heard of at least one salesperson who actually got his company's new and unannounced product price list from his competitors, not his own office.

MILLIONS SPENT ON SALES COMMUNICATIONS, BUT DOES ANY OF IT WORK?

I used to be the home office person sending out all that information. I spent millions of dollars each year writing, designing, and producing pieces of paper that were supposed to make my sales force more effective. Whether it ever worked was never questioned, it was just what we did. Today, fortunately, most of the wanton production of breast-beating brochures has been replaced by equally hyperbolic websites—less wasteful of forest products but no less time-consuming to produce and manage. Some organizations are relying on internal communities and internal Twitter accounts as well as services like Yammer and CoTweet to take advantage of the immediacy of Twitter.

Very few organizations know whether their sales communications are effective. Here's an example: A major computer manufacturer I recently worked with took a long look at its entire communication process, queried its sales force, and reduced the number of information sources from 50 to five. For real emergency news it now uses broadcast e-mail and voice mail. For urgent communications, there's a broadcast e-mail. For background information, it relies on an internal blog and website, and for broad-based strategic announcements it uses video conferencing.

Questions remained, however, about the usefulness of those sources. I helped the company design a research project that would not only determine whether the sales force liked the new approach, but also would correlate the flow of information against specific sales performance.

Here's how it worked: Just as the new communications strategy was being announced, we conducted a benchmark survey of the sales force. The study queried individual salespeople on their awareness and usage of the various communications vehicles and their understanding of the messages that the home office was trying to convey.

After six months of communicating via the new system, we again asked the members of the sales force about their awareness of the various vehicles and their understanding of the key messages. What was particularly exciting about this project was that we also knew who was selling what, how much, and how often. So, in addition to measuring overall satisfaction with the program, we used a secondary analysis to see if it was translating into actual sales. Using a list of the top 25 salespeople, we compared their sales performance, their survey responses, and the degree to which they used the new tools. The analysis showed that heavy users of the new online tools were more likely to be effective salespeople.

THE PROBLEM: MIXED MESSAGES, MIXED OBJECTIVES

Measuring relationships with salespeople gets more complex when you don't have a direct sales force and/or you have little control over the communications processes, such as happens if you're providing materials to franchisees or other channel partners. Any corporation that uses franchising as a way to distribute its product or service faces a dilemma unknown to its counterparts in other industries: How to maintain an overall consistent corporate image while allowing franchisees the freedom to develop programs that are customized to their local audiences?

In some ways, this problem strongly resembles what many U.S. companies face when expanding their communications efforts overseas. They need localized communications support while participating in an increasingly global community where they must maintain a consistent worldwide image. Balancing these two needs is difficult enough, but measuring the effectiveness of these types of programs can be even more so, especially in an era where the ubiquity of social media means that what happens in one franchise directly affects the entire corporate brand. Just ask Domino's Pizza what it thinks of YouTube (www.youtube.com/watch?v=hYomw1cLA2U).

One challenge arises from the mix of objectives. For example, one of the most frequently mentioned goals we hear is, "To reach our target audience with our key quality message." This goal is great as long as the target audiences are the same. But what if one franchisee targets seniors and the next targets college students? And what if the goal for corporate is to get new franchisees, and the goal for the franchisee is attracting better employees?

Another difficulty involves the mix of activities that franchisees can get involved with. What if one market has just undergone a natural disaster (all too common in the past few years) and the franchisee in that area is able to respond with a particularly effective relief effort? How will that impact a measurement program?

A third problem consists of getting buy-in from the huge cross-section of entrepreneurs who own the franchises. Notoriously independent, entrepreneurs stay up at night for radically different reasons than those that keep a typical corporate communications person awake. Franchisees worry about profitability, staffing, and on-time deliveries. They worry about what the bank and their customers think, and also about the consistency of their key messages, their budgets, and the opinions of the boss and the press.

THE SOLUTION: CONSISTENT MESSAGES

The key to an effective program lies in finding some common ground among all these different communities. That common ground must be a set of common objectives—not as difficult to find as you'd think. Consistency in advertising messages is a given; that's why national advertising campaigns exist. The challenge in PR is that you don't have as much control over what messages are really being communicated. And without a measurement program, you have even less. By quantifying what the media are saying about you and who is seeing those messages, some control over the image begins to be established—and at a far lower cost than a national advertising campaign.

So one objective that both the corporation and the franchisee can agree on is the need for consistent communication of a few nationwide corporate key messages. This supports the advertising program and makes everyone's dollars go further. If you have a good relationship with the franchisee, then the franchisee follows the guidelines you set and is consistent in its branding and its communications. If you have a bad relationship, then the franchisee will go its own way and introduce inconsistency in your branding efforts.

The criterion for success then becomes the percentage of articles that contain your key messages. This is determined by having an independent reader (not a PR person or a franchisee) analyze the media to determine what she takes away from each article.

OTHER MEASURES OF SUCCESS

- *More visibility than the competition.* It is critical that your publicity programs break through the clutter and get your name out more prominently than that of the competition. This doesn't just mean more articles. It means more mentions of the company or corporation name in headlines, captions, or other places of greater visibility.

  The criterion for success in this case could be sheer volume of coverage compared to the competition. An even better qualitative measure would be percent of articles featuring the company name in the headline. This figure then is compared to the percent of articles that mention the competition's name in the headlines.

- *Better image than the competition.* A major focus of any local promotional program is to increase community goodwill. The most direct means to measure this is by phone or intercept surveys of the local population, but such surveys can quickly become prohibitively expensive. A cost-effective alternative is to analyze local media coverage to determine how effectively publicity programs are generating goodwill.

  As part of the analysis, the reader should note the number of items (articles, transcripts, blog postings, threads, etc.) that portray the company or brand as a responsible corporate citizen. Your competition is no doubt conducting similar goodwill-generating programs, so you should include your top three or four competitors in the analysis and compare your results to theirs. It is very valuable to learn that your efforts are generating lots of goodwill in the community. But it's even *more* valuable to learn that your efforts are generating more than your competition.

- *Getting visibility for local franchisees.* Another element of a publicity program involves establishing company spokespeople as community leaders or reliable sources on topics of interest. This ensures opportunities for franchisees to increase their visibility in the local media. Obviously, if your spokesperson gets quoted more often than the owner of a competitive franchise, your program is more effective. It is critical, however, that spokespeople communicate the key corporate messages during these interviews. By tracking not just *who* is being quoted but *what* is being said, you can develop a very effective tool for improving your community relations. If the local folks are on message, then it implies that the local and national offices have a good relationship.

MEASURING WHAT MATTERS TO SALES

To measure your relationships with salespeople and franchisees, follow the seven steps outlined in Chapter 3, paying special attention to the measures of success just described. Before you begin to design any measurement program for yourself, be sure to review that chapter and work through the 10 Questions exercise in Chapter 2.

CASE STUDY: BLUE CROSS BLUE SHIELD CURES ITS IMAGE PROBLEM

Blue Cross Blue Shield is a good example of a strong national brand that is carried and promoted by very independent and diverse franchisees. We worked with one franchisee, Blue Cross Blue Shield of New Hampshire (BCBS-NH, now Anthem) to establish a benchmark for its communications efforts. To do this we conducted a competitive analysis of the company's public relations and public perceptions. First we analyzed all press coverage for BCBS-NH and its two key competitors. Then we interviewed two market segments, business decision makers and individual subscribers. We wanted to find out what issues were most important to them, where they got their information regarding health care, and what their current perceptions were of various companies.

Our findings revealed some serious problems in the company's overall image. Based on that information, BCBS-NH revamped its entire communications strategy and crafted new key messages that resulted in a significant turnaround for the company.

At the same time, the national Blue Cross Blue Shield Association was also reviewing its image and rolling out a new theme in a major new advertising campaign. BCBS-NH leveraged this increased national exposure by incorporating the national key messages into its own campaign. BCBS-NH's new awareness of potential subscribers' specific concerns enabled it to adjust key

(*continued*)

(Continued)

messages to clearly address those concerns while distinguishing itself from the competition. Because the research was already in hand, it was able to quickly develop a complementary strategy that played off the national theme and responded to the needs and perceptions of the local audience, thereby increasing its local visibility.

CHAPTER 13

MEASUREMENT FOR NONPROFITS

"One of the great mistakes is to judge policies and programs by their intentions rather than their results."

—Milton Friedman

Whether you run the local soup kitchen or a membership organization for civil engineers, maintaining good relationships with your members, volunteers, and donors is critical to your success. While relationships impact the bottom line in any organization, in the not-for-profit world relationships take on even greater importance.

In part, this comes from the fact that nonprofits are often seen as not really being businesses, even though many of them have multibillion dollar budgets. But the biggest reason that relationships matter to nonprofits is that the very nature of the operation relies on goodwill and volunteerism. Relationships are the foundation of the reputation and awareness that your PR and other marketing efforts have built. And without those relationships chances are no one would be donating or volunteering for anything. So if you don't have strong communal relationships with your constituencies, your organization will soon cease to survive. This is why it is critical to continuously measure the nature and efficacy of your relations.

NOT MEASURING IS NOT AN OPTION

Measurement and accountability have recently become more important than ever in the nonprofit sector. Here are three reasons why.

1. *Social Media.* The advent of social media has brought many new ways of reaching out to your community stakeholders, and without measurement you have no way of judging which will be most effective. Further complicating the environment, applications such as Ning, Mzinga, and other social groupware have provided nonprofits with easy no-cost or low-cost tools to create their own communities and stay in touch with their stakeholders. The good news is that not only are the varieties of communities growing, but so is our ability to measure them.

2. *Metrics.* In today's difficult financial environment nonprofits need to act more like *for*-profits in terms of measurement. Increasingly, executive directors and board members are being recruited from the for-profit sector, and they bring with them expectations that metrics will be available. Trustees are requiring detailed evaluation of programs and initiatives. There is greater competition among nonprofits for share of wallet. All of which increases pressure to measure results.

3. *Accountability.* At the same time, in a financially cautious world, donors and contributors are increasingly demanding accountability for their gifts. Trustees require detailed evaluation of programs and initiatives.

There's a perception out there, however, that only the biggest nonprofits can afford the money and person-power to really evaluate results. This is simply false. This chapter will describe the techniques and tools that will enable any organization to measure its success.

MEASURING RELATIONSHIPS WITH YOUR MEMBERSHIP

As a preliminary step, you need to understand where you are, what you know, and what you don't know. So conduct an audit of your organization's existing data. We're not talking about hiring an expensive external accounting firm, just understanding what data is already available:

- Attendance figures.
- Old awareness or attitude studies.
- Number of new members or donors acquired.
- Number of volunteers added.
- The return from your direct-mail campaigns, door-to-door solicitations, and fund raising events.
- What a donor is worth over a lifetime.

Now measurement proceeds roughly along the lines of the seven steps outlined in Chapter 3. Before you begin to design any measurement program for yourself, be sure to review that chapter, and work through the 10 Questions exercise in Chapter 2.

Step 1: Use Your Mission to Define Your Objectives

To measure what matters for your organization, your metrics must follow from your objectives, and your objectives must follow from your organization's mission. So, what is your organization's mission and reason for existence? What are your organization's definitions of success? What do those definitions say about the data you need to make better decisions in your job?

To help define objectives, one exercise we put our clients through is to have them complete a questionnaire that includes the following questions:

- What data do you need to make better decisions in your job?
- How do you define failure?

- How do you know if something is working?
- If someone says, "We're getting our butts kicked!" what does that mean?
- If someone says, "Congratulations! You're really kicking butt!" what does that look like?

Here's another exercise we lead our clients through: Suppose you were so successful that your boss gave you a 20 percent raise, a case of champagne, and an extra week off. What kind of achievement would prompt such a reward? What would then be different in your department and your organization?

The key to determining your measurement objectives is to push beyond the first level of aspirational goals to uncover the real bottom-line benefit that you want to achieve. And to be measurable, each objective requires a "by when" date and a "compared to what" benchmark. Typical objectives might be:

- Increase donations by a certain percentage over the coming year.
- Increase volunteers by a certain percentage over the coming year.
- Increase media coverage as compared to other nonprofits over the coming year.
- Increase trust and understanding of the organization's mission among the membership.

As an example, consider Habitat for Humanity. Habitat exists to build housing for people who can't afford it, with volunteers. That subordinate phrase is just as important as the main one. If all Habitat had to do was raise enough money to get contractors to build a house, that would be easy. The challenge is to raise enough money to build a house and then build it using volunteers. So Habitat can't just measure its success in terms of money, it needs to measure the number of volunteers as well.

Step 2: Identify and Prioritize Your Audiences

List the target stakeholders that your organization relates to, including both those that threaten and those that benefit your organization. Then, for each of those stakeholders, list how a good relationship can benefit your organization. Remember that your members are not a homogeneous bunch; whether it's an organization that meets once a month or a virtual network on Ning, there are new members, active members, dormant members, old members, nonrenewing members, former members, and not-yet-members that just need a nudge to get them to send in the form. You need to understand how a good relationship with each group of members can benefit your organization—and how a bad relationship can hurt it. Good relationships with long-standing members of your organization may bring in significant membership dues, but their value may be much greater if that's where your pool of leadership talent resides. Similarly, new members have value far beyond their dues, since they may help spread the word, be the most active volunteers, or become attendees at new events.

Now gather senior management and key marketing people within your organization and get them to prioritize the audiences. Put all the names up on a chart, and give everyone 10 colored sticky dots. Each dot is worth, say, $1,000,000 of budget (just think of it as Monopoly money). Ask all participants to spend their budgets by sticking their dots up next to the audiences they think most important. The audiences with the most dots are clearly the highest priority.

When you're thinking about metrics, remember that audiences do not live in a vacuum, nor do they hear only your messages. In today's society any one of your members is hit with some 6,000 messages a day from a wide variety of sources. Some, such as those delivered by advertising and direct mail, are messages you can control. But increasingly these channels are becoming less and less cost effective as the cost of mail goes up and the response rates go down. Others, like messages in traditional or social media, you may not be able to control, but if you can use them successfully your message can spread virally to a far larger audience.

A good measurement program looks at as many different influences as the budget allows. At the very least take into account what your stakeholders are seeing in the media; what they're exposed to online; what they're hearing from you; what they're taking away in terms of impressions, awareness, or understanding; and ultimately, what actions they take—renew membership, get friends to join, volunteer, and so on. All these various influences on members affect your relationships with them. So it's necessary to understand and quantify those influences if you want to understand why the relationship is improving or deteriorating.

Step 3: Establish a Benchmark

If I tell you that 35 percent of your members think your organization is the best thing that ever happened to them, you don't know if that's good or bad. It could be bad that 65 percent of the audience doesn't feel that way. But on the other hand, if only 15 percent of them thought a competing organization was worth joining, then 35 percent looks like a great number.

Measurement is a comparative tool, and while you can always compare your results over time, it is far preferable to identify a competitor, perceived competitor, or peer organization with which you might be competing for share of wallet or share of mind or loyalty. Unlike in corporate America, cooperation is common among nonprofits, and organizations can partner on the research in order to have something to compare their results to. Whether you select competing organizations or peer organizations, try to limit the number of entities in any given study to no more than five. Three is ideal; anything more than five becomes unwieldy.

Nothing is more effective in making a case for business changes than showing that a local competitor has a more cost-effective program than yours. Comparisons between organizations have a downside, of course. No two organizations are alike, so if you are running a museum and the only other nonprofit in town is a church, the results will probably not be comparable, given the different audiences. In such a case you would be better off finding another museum in a similarly sized city with which to share and compare data.

Comparing results between departments is also tricky. While such comparisons do, in fact, drive individuals to excel, you can easily misinterpret data that exaggerates differences between departments and exacerbates internecine tensions. However, it is important to compare cost effectiveness between departments. Your direct-mail department may seem to be the most effective, but if it takes them two extra people and twice the budget, you need to decide if the extra expenditure is worth the cost.

Step 4: Pick Your Metrics

Your metrics are your numbers, the data points you collect to quantify progress on the objectives you developed in Step 1. The most important thing to remember about any measurement program is that you become what you measure. Therefore, you want to define metrics that will help you become what you want to become. The metrics that you define as important will be the ones that everyone in the organization will attempt to achieve, so getting them right at the start is crucial.

For example, if your mission is to enact or defeat legislation, the metric might be "number of bills passed," or some measure of the degree to which your point of view is communicated in the media. If you're trying to engage people with your website, you might want to make some measure of web traffic a key metric. Lots of organizations say they want to build community, but just having a community isn't the end result. You build community because it encourages brand loyalty, reduces churn, or gets more people to take action on your behalf.

Here are the objectives mentioned in Step 1, and corresponding metrics that would be appropriate:

- Increase donations by a certain percentage over the coming year: Dollar amount of donations per month or per year.
- Increase volunteers by a certain percentage over the coming year: Number of new volunteers per time period, total new volunteers each time period.
- Increase media coverage as compared to other nonprofits over the coming year: Mentions, key messages, and/or tone as compared to that of the competition by time period.
- Increase trust and understanding of the organization's mission among the membership: Change in scores on a survey of the membership.

Step 5: Pick a Measurement Tool

Depending on what you're measuring, you will need to analyze your media coverage or survey your membership, or preferably both. See Chapter 2 for more on measurement tools and costs.

Use Content Analysis to Measure Activity, Sentiment, and Messaging
To learn what the world is seeing and hearing about your organization, you use media content analysis to quantify your image as portrayed in print, blogs, TV, and any media that is important to your audiences. You don't have to analyze the world, just those publications, blogs, channels, or media sources that are most important to your audience. Once you've established a key media list, make sure you have access to all items in those media outlets. This will be either via your own subscriptions, via a content collection service, or, for traditional media, clipping services.

Every item should be read for the following criteria:

- The main subject of the item.
- The type of item it is—opinion, feature story, Q&A, letter to the editor, and so on.

- The visibility of the organization within the item. Was your organization the focal point or did it just receive a minor mention?
- Who, if anyone, was quoted in the item and what was his or her affiliation?
- The tonality: Did it leave the reader more or less likely to join your organization?
- The type of media in which the item appeared: TV, magazine, business press, personal blog, corporate blog, Twitter, and so on.
- Which, if any, key messages were communicated?
- How were the organization and its peers positioned on key issues such as "good value for the money," "effective advocate for the industry," or "responsiveness?"

Typical metrics might be:

- *Percentage of exposure containing key messages.* By analyzing the media (print, radio, TV, or Internet) you can see if your messages appeared. (This is a good place to put your interns to work.) Use the audited circulation figures of the media in which your messages appeared to determine the number of opportunities to see your messages. You can also rank the exposure on a scale of most likely to be seen to least likely to be seen. Studies show that if a message appears in a headline, callout, or caption, it is most likely to be seen and remembered.
- *Cost per message communicated.* Once you've tallied the opportunities to see your messages (OTS), you can calculate the cost of disseminating the messages via advertising vs. underwriting vs. PR, or whatever methods you employ. Divide the budget for the program, launch or period by the number of OTS that have occurred during the same period. This calculates the cost per message communicated. If you want to make the number comparable to cost per thousand opportunities to see the message (CPM, the common advertising calculation), you will need to multiply that number by 1000. You can use cost per message communicated or CPM to compare your PR efforts to similar programs such as advertising or direct mail. This will help you

decide where and how you want to disseminate messages in the future. One drawback to this method is that accurate OTS for social media are not always available.

- *Level of message penetration.* If your *raison d'être* is educating the public or getting your messages across, you not only need to know if your idea was seen by your audience, you also need to determine whether they heard it. We all know it's not enough to merely get messages out there, what we really need to evaluate is whether anyone heard them or if they changed anyone's opinions.

But doing pre- and post-awareness surveys is too expensive, right? *Wrong.* Think creatively. Can you build a test into your website or next event to gauge people's awareness? Give them a prize for getting three right answers. Or create a passport system for which they have to answer questions and get their passport stamped to signify that they know one of your messages.

You don't need to spend a lot of money to conduct this research. Virtually all the content is available via Google News, and a simple Excel spreadsheet will work just fine to manage and track the data. Additionally, many organizations, including my own, offer nonprofit rates.

Use Surveys to Measure What People Think about You   To measure perceptions you need to do a survey. In our opinion, the most reliable way to measure relationships with your members is to conduct an in-depth survey using the Grunig Relationship Survey. See Chapter 4 for a more detailed discussion and Appendix 1 for a list of the actual questions to put in the questionnaire.

This survey can be conducted in person, by phone, or online. Online surveys are most organizations' first choice these days because they are inexpensive and easy to do. Online surveys by companies such as SurveyMonkey and Zoomerang are available free and are widely used. The trick is to make sure you have a good e-mail list of your members. Alternatively, you can use free polling apps such as Vizu or PollDaddy that are easy to install on your blog and give you instant feedback on a topic.

In-person polling will probably give you the most accurate responses, but can be very time consuming and is therefore the most expensive alternative. Phone surveys are increasingly expensive in the advent of Do Not Call rules. They are also increasingly limited in their accuracy; many people no longer have landlines, and the percentage of cell phone-only households grows every year.

Other low-cost ways to gather data include:

- *Board-administered constituency questionnaires.* Give your board members a survey and ask them to get feedback and ideas from their peers and colleagues. Explain why this data will help your endeavor. If you have 10 board members and each interviews 10 friends, you've got enough data to yield reliable statistics, as long as you don't try to slice and dice the numbers too narrowly.
- *Use a booth at a local festival.* If there is a local or regional festival at which your organization has a booth, create a questionnaire that people have to fill out in order to win a prize. The people staffing the booth should encourage visitors to fill out the questionnaire, but they must be consistent about when during the visit they ask. If visitors fill out the questionnaire *before* they've talked to anyone, you will get more off-the-cuff comments, whereas if visitors consistently fill it out *after* they've talked to booth staff, you'll learn what information they've taken away.
- *Attendee or constituency surveys.* At least once a year, include a survey in a mailing or distribute it to attendees at an event. Make sure you ask the same questions year after year so you can gauge changes in perceptions over time.

Measuring Behavioral Change Member behavior can take many forms: renewals, donations, web traffic, e-mail responses, phone calls, attendance at trade shows, votes, and so on. All are relatively easy to measure once you have a tracking system in place. The key is to keep track of them on a monthly basis, and then compare the results to your media activity and ideally to the attitude research. With sufficient data you will be able to see correlations between activities in the media, communications with your membership, and behavioral outcomes.

We recommend one or more of the following metrics:

- *Cost per donor acquired.* Count the number of new donors each month. Divide that number into the total amount (including salaries) that you spend trying to get those donors.
- *Cost per volunteer acquired.* Track the number of new volunteers you've signed up each month. Divide that number into the total amount (including salaries) that you spent in recruitment efforts.
- *Cost per contribution:* For every solicitation you send out, how much revenue comes in? The trick is to calculate not just the cost of the solicitation itself (a direct-mail piece, for instance), but the labor and marketing efforts that accompany it. Direct-mail experts know these numbers cold, so if you have one on your board, enlist his help.
- *Cost per attendee.* If your nonprofit or event is designed to bring more people through the door, you need to be counting traffic on a daily or weekly basis. The key is to track that traffic against other marketing and communications activities. For instance, if you double the resources you devote to PR, does attendance go up proportionately? Even more revealing, if you cut back on advertising or PR efforts, does attendance decline? With sufficient amounts of data, you can calculate what it costs to get someone through your doors.
- *Return on investment of a website.* If you are taking donations from your website, calculate the cost of the site and its maintenance and subtract that from the amount of the donations coming in. Do this weekly or monthly, then when you make changes to your website you can see how it affects the ROI.

Measuring Results During a Crisis   The one situation that doesn't fall neatly into the above criteria is a crisis. (See Chapter 11 for more on crisis measurement.) Whatever the actual crisis event, the measure becomes quite simple: How quickly does it go away, and how long does anyone remember it? Both questions are relatively easy to answer. For the first question, begin tracking media coverage on day one. If you have the time and resources, track the tone of the coverage and messages communicated. If not, just count the number of clips on day one, day two, and so on, until there are no more clips left to track. If your crisis is well managed, the worst coverage should happen during the first week and decline after that. If the crisis spins out of control, you'll be able to see it very quickly.

Step 6: Analyze Results and Make Changes

Remember that you want to measure your failures as well as your successes. If you don't know what didn't work, you are doomed to repeat it. Have the confidence to point out what doesn't work; this conveys the message that you are managing budgets well and are willing to make judgments based on facts, not emotions.

Evaluation is not something that gets done once and put away. It should be an ongoing process so you can examine the impact of a variety of elements over time. For instance: Does an event work better at a particular time of the year? You'll only know if you are looking at results over the entire year.

Once you have your member relationship measurement program in place, make it a regular, ongoing part of your communications process. When the data comes in, learn from your successes and mistakes, make changes, and then see the results in the next reporting period.

One caveat: Make sure the data is available when you need it. If you do all your budgeting and planning in August, having data at the end of the calendar year does you no good whatsoever. Or, if you know you are going to be writing a big grant application, plan your research so you have the data available just before you write it. The data and analysis should be fresh just as you need it.

CHAPTER 14

MEASURE WHAT MATTERS IN HIGHER EDUCATION: HOW TO GET AN A IN MEASUREMENT

"No longer is it acceptable to hide poor performance. Measuring is the gateway to success."
—George W. Bush, on No Child Left Behind legislation

In case you hadn't noticed, crass commercialism has arrived at the door of academia. I'm sure that's what many academics think of the emphasis on marketing that has been sweeping through campuses across America. Even before the recession sent millions of people back to school in search of new job skills, institutions of higher learning were being pressured to think more like businesses. Universities and colleges are more aggressively marketing to alumni, new students, parents, and faculty. This increased effort has generated a requisite increase in accountability for the money being spent.

More and more educational institutions are realizing that managing their reputations is critical to their survival. You can have the best faculty in the world, but if no one knows it you're not going to attract students. And, as we know, in order to manage you need to measure. So measurement is making it onto to-do lists of communications and public affairs officers in colleges and universities of all shapes and sizes.

UNIVERSITY FLUNKS MEASUREMENT: MILLIONS IN FUNDING LOST AND PRESIDENT RESIGNS

Here's a true story about the vital importance of measuring what matters in academia. Once upon a time not very long ago, there was a state university in a small town in New England. Both the university and the town needed new soccer fields. One of the university's alumni, a successful local entrepreneur, stepped forward and offered to donate $6 million so the university could build them. A site was selected, town officials were notified, and the university assumed it would soon be hosting soccer tournaments.

Now the university was a venerable institution, and it took care to maintain its reputation of quality and prestige by communicating about itself to the world. But it failed to understand that some very important changes had been occurring in the town. For much of the university's history, most of the people who lived in the town year round either worked for the university or had family or friends involved there. Over recent decades, however, rising real estate prices and property taxes had forced much of the faculty and staff out of town. Their houses were bought up by retirees and commuters who had no particular connection with the university. So the town's permanent residents, who had once formed a sympathetic constituency, gradually changed into an inactive, disengaged public. The university's reputation with this new public was still fine, but the strength of its connection with them was now different—unmeasured and untested.

Several years before the soccer fields were planned, the university had embarked on another large construction project, a 6,000-seat sports and entertainment arena. The university, a tax-exempt and local zoning-exempt state entity, chose to simply notify the townspeople of its plans. It completely failed to anticipate that the town's permanent residents might object to potential parking problems or the absence of any local tax benefits. As a result, many townspeople felt railroaded by the university and town officials, and, after a contentious political campaign, replaced the town leadership.

Let's skip ahead a couple of years to the soccer fields proposal. The university, despite its strong public relations department, had been making no effort to understand the concerns of its constituencies. It was unaware that a good part of the town's permanent residents had become well-organized and were potentially quite hostile. When the university announced its new construction project, the reaction was swift, noisy, and disastrous. The citizens' group, now 2,000 members strong, got the attention of the statewide media, and used e-mail and their Listserv to ensure that every university trustee and every politician heard their complaints.

Less than two months after being announced, the proposed soccer fields were cancelled, the $6-million gift was rejected, and the university president stepped down. It was a stiff price to pay for misunderstanding one's publics. What went wrong?

Some argue that the university should have just paid more attention to its PR. And it should have. But the university's biggest problem was that it failed to measure what really mattered.

KEY CONSIDERATIONS: MULTIPLE AUDIENCES = MULTIPLE GOALS = MULTIPLE METRICS

There are several interesting elements that make research and evaluation unique in an academic environment:

- *Everyone is an expert.* For starters, you're dealing with people who do research for a living. This means they will challenge your statistics and your calculations in ways that very few people in the corporate world ever will. They live and die by the accuracy of their data and their ability to reason from it, so yours better be just as accurate and just as defensible as any of the masters' theses they see. So watch your r factors when you're doing those correlations. http://en.wikipedia.org/wiki/Correlation_and_dependence

- *They have masses of data at their fingertips.* Unlike in corporate America, where most of my clients run screaming from the room the moment the data gets too deep, in the university environment people love their data. And they love to have lots of it. Need to know the average SAT score of every freshman class for the past five years? They've got it. Need data on how many alumnae come back for every football game? They've got it. And it's not just the professors. I've spoken to a number of university presidents and they can rattle off statistics like you wouldn't believe. The good news is that if you want to determine how the football team's record impacts the number and quality of student applications, the data is there.

- *Under every ivy leaf hides another audience.* An element that makes measuring in an educational environment a bit more challenging is the number of specific audiences you need to address: faculty, staff, students, parents, alumnae, town officials, state and national politicians, and the list goes on. It's not necessarily longer than for your average multinational corporation, but the needs and interests are very different. In a recent presentation at the Whittemore School of Business and Economics at the University of New Hampshire, Steve Reno, the chancellor of the University System of New Hampshire, listed 10 different stakeholders with some six dozen different agendas that he needs to juggle on a daily basis. What this means for measurement is that you've got a lot of listening to do and a lot of possible issues to keep track of.

- Each institution has its own goals and metrics, but certain KPIs cross all institutions. The head of almost any educational institution can give you certain basic measures of success off the top of his or her head. These include their ranking in the *US News and World Report* survey, their alumnae donor rate, their retention rate, their average applicant SAT score, and their discount rate (the difference between full tuition and what students are really paying). These are the stats that university presidents live and die by.

- *There is really only one goal.* The goal of any university communications program is to contribute to the education of the students. That is the bottom line. That's why you need to raise the money, get the publicity, boost the rankings, or have that press conference. Ultimately, if you're not educating students, the institution will cease to exist.

- *No matter how successful the football team, you're still in a nonprofit environment.* Few educational institutions budget anywhere near enough for communications and/or marketing/public affairs, never mind measurement. The good news is that many of the metrics are readily available, so it doesn't necessarily have to cost a lot of money to put a measurement system in place.

CASE STUDY: DISTANCE LEARNING USES CREATIVE DATA COMPARISONS TO GENERATE POWERFUL MEASURES OF SUCCESS

The person in charge of distance learning for a state university system was struggling to develop measures of success that would show the true value of his division to the state. He could readily count the number of people enrolled in distance learning programs, but that wasn't convincing the legislature or even his managers that the program was really worth the state's investment.

However, when he probed a bit deeper into the data, he found that 75 percent of those enrolled went into higher paying high-tech jobs. Clearly, the program was turning out better educated and better trained potential employees. This fact would

(continued)

(*Continued*)

have great appeal to any company considering relocating to his state. In fact, the State Office of Economic Development knew from its own data that the presence of an educated workforce was the number one driving factor for companies considering relocation to the state. Moreover, he also discovered that the state typically allocated up to $10,000 per job in tax incentives to entice companies to move to the state.

Ah-ha! Using these figures he could compare the amount the state spent on the distance learning program to the amount spent on tax incentives. Turns out that, as measured by the cost to attract new business to the state, the distance learning program was much less expensive than tax incentives. And so distance learning found a very valuable measure of success.

FIVE STEPS FOR GETTING AN A IN MEASUREMENT

The step-by-step procedure described below follows roughly the steps outlined in Chapter 3. Before you begin to design any measurement program for yourself, be sure to review that chapter and work through the 10 Questions exercise.

Step 1: Identify and Prioritize Your Audiences

The first step is to understand the psychographics and characteristics of all the various audiences involved, and they are anything but homogeneous. Remember that each of your multiple constituencies have different needs, wants, expectations, and desires. There are new students/faculty/alumnae, old students/faculty/alumnae, nonrenewing students/faculty/alumnae, and former students/faculty/alumnae, just to name a few. So figure out just who it is you need to listen to, talk to, and manage relationships with.

Typical audiences within the academic environment include:

- Faculty
- Staff
- Deans
- Alumnae
- Students
- Parents
- Prospective students
- Parents of prospective students
- Donors
- Federal government
- State government
- Local elected officials and the local community
- Local media
- National media
- Trade media

The next step in the process is to get all your various "bosses" to agree on a set of priorities. To do that, you need to understand how a good relationship with each constituency benefits your institution and how a bad relationship can hurt it. For instance, students are the sort of people who, when they are unhappy, will immediately tell Facebook and the rest of the world about their unhappiness. Thus a bad relationship with students will have a relatively quick and negative impact on the image of your institution. So make a list of all your constituencies and next to each one list the benefits that a great relationship with that group brings to your institution.

Then you need to gather the senior leadership team and key communications people within your institution and get them to prioritize the audiences. The way we do it is to list the audiences on a whiteboard and then pass out 10 colored sticky dots to each person. Each dot is worth $100,000 of the communications budget. We then ask all participants to spend their budgets in the ways that they think are most appropriate. The audience with the most dots is clearly the most important.

Step 2: Define Your Objectives and Get Everyone on the Same Page

The important thing to remember about any measurement program is that you become what you measure. Those metrics that you define as important will be the ones that everyone will attempt to achieve, so getting them right is crucial. One exercise we put our clients through is to ask them to close their eyes and imagine their president delivering a case of Dom Perignon to their desk in gratitude for the best year ever. Then I ask them what has changed, or what is it that they accomplished that is different from a year ago.

Another way to approach this is to go back to your list of the benefits a good relationship brings to the institution and see if any of them would make good objectives. Then consider what metrics are suited to those objectives. For example, if your institution's number one priority is to grow the student body while maintaining academic excellence, then typical metrics would be media visibility and average SAT score of applicants. You would use these to investigate the correlation between improving messaging and/or desirable coverage and whether you are getting a higher caliber of applications. If your mission is to build the endowment, then the metric might be the percentage of alumni who donate or the increase in average alumni donor amount. If you rely on the Web to attract applicants, you might want to make web traffic and application downloads a key metric.

When you're thinking about metrics, remember that audiences do not live in a vacuum nor do they only hear your messages. In today's society any one of your students, faculty, alumnae, and so on is bombarded with some 6,000 messages a day from a wide variety of sources. Some, like advertising and direct mail, you can control. Others, like the media, you can't. A good measurement program looks at as many different influences as the budget allows. At the very least you should take into account what your students, faculty, alumnae, and other audiences are seeing in the media; what they're exposed to online; what they're hearing from you; what they're taking away in terms of impressions, awareness, or understanding; and ultimately what actions they take. For example, do they download applications and brochures or make a donation? All these various influences affect your relationship. So it's necessary to understand and quantify those influences if you want to understand why the relationship is improving or declining.

Step 3: Establish a Benchmark

If I tell you that 35 percent of alumnae donate to your university, what does that tell you? It says that 65 percent aren't donating—but it doesn't tell you whether that is a good number or a bad number. Do your peer institutions have higher or lower rates of alumni giving? Is your rate of alumni giving going up or down? Since measurement is a comparative tool, you need to figure out what you are benchmarking your results against. It could be a peer institution or a competitive institution. Institutions may be able to partner on the research in order to have something to compare their results to.

Whether you select competing institutions or peer institutions, try to limit the number of entities in any given study to no more than five. Three is ideal; anything more than five becomes unwieldy.

Step 4: Pick a Measurement Tool and Collect Data

Depending on what you're measuring you will either need to analyze your media coverage or survey your students, faculty, alumnae, and other audiences. Or preferably do both.

Measure What the Media Is Saying about You   Media analysis will tell you what information your audiences are exposed to and whether your communications efforts are getting out the information you want them exposed to. You don't have to analyze the world, just those sources that are most important to your audiences. So if faculty is your priority audience, you need to make sure you're measuring academic journals as well as mainstream media. If students are the number one audience, remember that this group consumes very little mainstream media and gets most of its information from online sources. So you should be monitoring forums like Facebook and media like Twitter. Once you've established a key media list, make sure you have access to all articles in those media outlets, either via your own subscriptions or via a clipping service.

Don't do your own reading and coding of articles. You will be far too quick to spot a key message (particularly your own) and are much more sensitive to reporters' opinions than are normal human beings. Ideally, you should find a member of your target audience—a student, faculty member, or prospective parent—to analyze the media.

To accurately gauge the impact of your media efforts, you should analyze all mentions of your institution as well as your peer institutions for the following criteria:

- The main subject.
- The type of article it is: opinion, feature story, Q&A, letter to the editor, and so on.
- The visibility of the institution within the article: Was your institution the focal point, or did it just receive a minor mention?
- The visibility of individual departments, subjects, or initiatives.
- Who, if anyone, was quoted in the article?
- The tonality: Did it leave the reader more or less likely to join your institution?
- The type of media in which the article appeared: TV, magazine, business press, and so forth.
- What, if any, messages were communicated?

- How was the institution (and its peers) positioned on key issues such as "good value for the money," "quality of education," or "responsiveness?"

Measure Social Media in the Academic Environment   Research has shown that social media is an important tool for academic admissions departments, and in many cases it is more commonly used in academia than in the corporate world (Barnes & Mattson, "The Game Has Changed: College Admissions Outpace Corporations in Embracing Social Media" www1.umassd.edu/cmr/studiesresearch/cmrblogstudy3.pdf). In this case, 88 percent of responding admissions departments said that social media was very important or somewhat important to their marketing/recruitment strategy. Sixty-one percent said that they used social media. Specifically, 33 percent used blogs, 29 percent used social networking, and 19 percent used video.

University communications increasingly is relying on social media to communicate to students, alumni, and even parents. Worth noting is that the fastest growing segment on Facebook is women over 50, so don't think that social media only applies to student communications. Clearly parents—and even grandparents—are using it to stay in touch with their children, and presumably, the institutions where their children are going to school.

Social media provides both a wonderful opportunity and a potential liability to your communications and marketing efforts. Many faculty members are subject matter experts, and you want to leverage their expertise and their blogs to promote your institution's brand. Their blogs frequently end up high in search results, so they offer excellent opportunities. However, it is important to follow and track what the public is seeing from such institutional blogs. Our research shows that institutional faculty or departmental blogs are seldom on message (www.sncr.org/wp-content/uploads/2009/11/ONLINEREPMGT09ENTRIES_ar.pdf).

The most important aspect of measuring your image and relationships in social media is to recognize the plethora of different channels. Typically we recommend tracking your image (and those of your peers) in the following channels:

- Social bookmarking sites like Digg
- Facebook
- YouTube
- Second Life
- Twitter
- Institutional blogs
- External blogs
- Online news sources

To provide a way to compare the nature of the conversations in all those different channels you need a standard set of mention types. Review the 27 types of conversations listed in Chapter 4, and use them to organize your data.

Measure What People Think   To measure what people are thinking about your institution, you need to field a survey. To understand how your audiences feel about your relationship with them, the best tool to use is the Grunig Relationship Survey, which we describe in detail in Chapter 4 and Appendix 1. The questionnaire can be administered in person, by telephone, or by e-mail. In person will probably get the most accurate responses, but it is very time consuming and therefore the most expensive alternative. Phone surveys are probably the best way to get a sufficient quantity of reliable data, but they, too, can be expensive. Online surveys by companies like SurveyMonkey and Zoomerang are essentially free, and thus can be done very inexpensively. The trick is to make sure you have good e-mail lists for your various audiences.

Measure Behavior

Since there are so many different constituencies within the academic environment, you will need many different tools to measure their behavioral changes. The good news is that social media provides an excellent way to measure actual engagement with your brand. Student and alumni behavior can be measured by using web analytics to judge engagement and participation in institution-sponsored online programs. Inquiries and requests for information and applications are good indicators of success among prospects and parents.

Good ways to judge your relationship with your faculty are the extent of their cooperation with your public affairs folks and the frequency of their interviews and quotes. All are relatively easy to measure once you have a tracking system in place. The key is to keep track of them on a monthly basis and then compare the results to your media activity and ideally to the survey research. With sufficient data you will be able to see correlations between activities in the media, communications with your audiences, and behavioral outcomes.

Step 5: Analyze the Data, Glean Insight, Make Changes, and Measure Again

All the data in the world is simply trivia if you can't draw some conclusions from it. So when the data is in, look for trends over time; for differences between new students, faculty, and alumnae and old students, faculty, and alumnae; and for differences between males and females. By all means look most carefully at the bad news and the failures, because that is where you will learn the most.

Once you have your relationship measurement program in place, you need to make it a regular, ongoing part of your communications process. When the data comes in, you learn from your mistakes, make changes, and then see the results in the next reporting process. One caveat: Make sure the data is available when you need it. If you do all your budgeting and planning in August, having end of year data does you no good whatsoever. The data should be fresh just as you are beginning your planning sessions.

Epilogue
Whither Measurement?

"The best way to predict the future is to invent it."

—Alan Kay

Four years ago in *Measuring Public Relationships*, I wrote on the question of "whither measurement?" Back then, no one had heard of Twitter, Hulu, or the iPhone. Facebook was just for students, and there were about 1,000 more newspapers and magazines on the market. PR was mostly about pitching stories to top-tier media and managing the message. Automated content analysis was still in its infancy and dashboards were all the rage.

At the time I predicted that:

The future of public relations lies in the development of relationships, and the future of measurement lies in the accurate analysis of those relationships. Counting impressions will become increasingly irrelevant while measuring relationships and reputation will become ever more important. Smart communicators are already pushing beyond measuring outputs and outtakes and learning to measure the feelings, perceptions, and relationships that they generate. What people think of you, how they perceive your actions, and what they do as a result of those perceptions are truly the metrics of the future.

Which goes to prove that my philosophy of life still holds true: You're never wrong, you're just early.

So, to approach this epilogue in a truly social way, I posed the "wither measurement?" question to my merry band of Twitter followers. Here are a few of the responses:

- From @HTOsborne: "It goeth on to answer the question 'so whatith?'. . .?"
- From @aliciakan: "Wither goes measurement? To universities where the course Communications ROI is required, not elective, for all marketing majors."
- From @ellenhoenig: "Measurement as valuable and relatable as content itself?"

They are all right.

@HTOsborne's point is the most important. If PR pros just use measurement to justify their existence and not to answer the question "So what?" measurement will die a long, slow, and painful death in their organizations. Management is not going to pay for anything that only justifies but instead will pay for research that helps them figure out how to make their programs better—and that necessitates an answer to the "So what?" question.

And the corollary is @ellenhoenig's point that measurement has to be seen as critical to the enterprise. Measurement and the data it produces can and should shape the content and the actions and the strategies formulated by every organization. All you creative types out there take note. I'm not saying that creativity won't be valued, but creativity should be shaped at least in part by what the customer wants and needs, and this reality will increasingly shape content going forward. It's been happening in the online advertising world for years; now it's just going to move over into PR.

And @aliciakan is dead-on when she suggests that universities are the key to measurement's future. (And PR's as well, for that matter.) Universities are already turning out communications professionals who understand correlations and the math and theory behind web analytics. And when those graduates hit the marketplace they are going to look at the antiquated measurement practices of their bosses and cry, "OMG WTF!"

The next generation of PR professionals is going to expect to use data to make better decisions, and they will understand how to interpret it. They will approach measurement from the assumption that integration is possible, and sooner or later they will replace those who see PR as a siloed ivory tower that needs to be defended.

If anything, with the advent of one-on-one connections between PR people and customers in the social media space, relationships will continue to be more important than ever. More and more organizations are pinning results to engagement—which is just another way to say "building relationships." The problem is that the developers who drive our industry aren't focused on real relationship metrics based on proven components of relationships. Instead, they are cooking up engagement simulations and wasting our time trying to translate friends, followers, and retweets into "engagement." Perhaps they'll succeed, eventually. In the meantime, I think the biggest change in measurement will be the increasing reliance on web metrics as a way of showing that we actually get our stakeholders to do something.

Will we see a time, as I predicted four years ago, when:

> ... increased sophistication in text-mining software, and natural language programming ... will mean that we will soon be able to pull meaning out of that big bucket o' words called new media, and communicators will be able to automatically determine whether their messages are going out and just how they are being positioned.

Yes, we will see that time, but not in the next few years. Developers of those automated systems are too focused on getting sentiment right, which I predict they will do, but not to a degree to which their results can't be challenged by a CMO.

In the meantime, humans who can tell you the "so what?"—who can shape the questions, interpret the data, and make the decisions— will still drive both measurement and the communications industry. Let's face it, who will find trust, commitment, or satisfaction in communal relationships with a computer?

KDP

APPENDIX 1
THE GRUNIG RELATIONSHIP SURVEY

The following survey statements, which in this book we call the Grunig Relationship Survey, are from "Guidelines for Measuring Relationships in Public Relations" by Dr. Linda Childers Hon and Dr. James E. Grunig, copyright 1999, Institute for Public Relations. This paper is relatively short and available at no cost from the Institute for Public Relations website (www.instituteforpr.org/files/uploads/Guidelines_Measuring_Relationships.pdf). It presents a bracing argument "... that the fundamental goal of public relations is building relationships with an organization's key constituencies." It discusses the underlying dimensions of relationships (trust, control mutuality, commitment, satisfaction, communal, and exchange), and it provides a straightforward tool to measure them, in the form of the questionnaire below.

We present these statements here to encourage your further interest and to demonstrate the relative simplicity of the technique, rather than as an actual working reference. If you are going to use these statements to measure relationships, then you must refer to the paper for the correct procedure and helpful tips. (For instance, you do not need to use all the questions.) We discuss the use of this questionnaire in Chapter 4. For more detail on administering the survey, see this follow-up paper by Jim Grunig, "Qualitative Methods for Assessing Relationships Between Organizations and Publics" (www.instituteforpr.org/files/uploads/2002_AssessingRelations.pdf).

223

The following are agree/disagree statements. Respondents are asked to use a 1 to 7 scale to indicate the extent to which each item listed describes their relationship with a particular organization. The statements marked "(Reversed)" present the relationship in a negative, rather than positive, light.

TRUST

1. This organization treats people like me fairly and justly.

2. Whenever this organization makes an important decision, I know it will be concerned about people like me.

3. This organization can be relied on to keep its promises.

4. I believe that this organization takes the opinions of people like me into account when making decisions.

5. I feel very confident about this organization's skills.

6. This organization has the ability to accomplish what it says it will do.

7. Sound principles seem to guide this organization's behavior.

8. This organization does not mislead people like me.

9. I am very willing to let this organization make decisions for people like me.

10. I think it is important to watch this organization closely so that it does not take advantage of people like me. (Reversed)

11. This organization is known to be successful at the things it tries to do.

CONTROL MUTUALITY

1. This organization and people like me are attentive to what each other say.

2. This organization believes the opinions of people like me are legitimate.

3. In dealing with people like me, this organization has a tendency to throw its weight around. (Reversed)

4. This organization really listens to what people like me have to say.

5. The management of this organization gives people like me enough say in the decision-making process.

6. When I have an opportunity to interact with this organization, I feel that I have some sense of control over the situation.

7. This organization won't cooperate with people like me. (Reversed)

8. I believe people like me have influence on the decision makers of this organization.

COMMITMENT

1. I feel that this organization is trying to maintain a long-term commitment to people like me.

2. I can see that this organization wants to maintain a relationship with people like me.

3. There is a long-lasting bond between this organization and people like me.

4. Compared to other organizations, I value my relationship with this organization more.

5. I would rather work together with this organization than not.

6. I have no desire to have a relationship with this organization. (Reversed)

7. I feel a sense of loyalty to this organization.

8. I could not care less about this organization. (Reversed)

SATISFACTION

1. I am happy with this organization.

2. Both the organization and people like me benefit from the relationship.

3. Most people like me are happy in their interactions with this organization.

4. Generally speaking, I am pleased with the relationship this organization has established with people like me.

5. Most people enjoy dealing with this organization.

6. The organization fails to satisfy the needs of people like me. (Reversed)

7. I feel people like me are important to this organization.

8. In general, I believe that nothing of value has been accomplished between this organization and people like me. (Reversed)

COMMUNAL RELATIONSHIPS

1. This organization does not especially enjoy giving others aid. (Reversed)

2. This organization is very concerned about the welfare of people like me.

3. I feel that this organization takes advantage of people who are vulnerable. (Reversed)

4. I think that this organization succeeds by stepping on other people. (Reversed)

5. This organization helps people like me without expecting anything in return.

6. I don't consider this to be a particularly helpful organization. (Reversed)

7. I feel that this organization tries to get the upper hand. (Reversed)

EXCHANGE RELATIONSHIPS

1. Whenever this organization gives or offers something to people like me, it generally expects something in return.

2. Even though people like me have had a relationship with this organization for a long time, it still expects something in return whenever it offers us a favor.

3. This organization will compromise with people like me when it knows that it will gain something.

4. This organization takes care of people who are likely to reward the organization.

Appendix 2
Measurement Resources

Books on Public Relations and Public Relations Research

Broom, Glen M., and David M. Dozier. *Using Research in Public Relations: Applications to Program Management*. Englewood Cliffs, NJ: Prentice Hall, 1990, 1996.

Grunig, James E., and Larissa A. Gruning. *Excellence in Public Relations and Communication Management*. Hillsdale, NJ: Lawrence Erlbaum Associates, 1992.

Grunig, James A., Larissa A. Grunig, and David M. Dozier. *Excellent Public Relations and Effective Organizations*. Hillsdale, NJ: Lawrence Erlbaum Associates, 2002.

Lindenmann, Walter K. *Public Relations Research for Planning and Evaluation* (available from the IPR website, www.instituteforpr.org).

Stacks, Don W. *Primer of Public Relations Research*. New York: The Guilford Press, 2002.

Two useful resources for qualitative and quantitative research techniques (both available from the Advertising Research Foundation, 432 Park Avenue South, New York, NY 10016):
- *Guidelines for the Public Use of Market and Opinion Research.*
- *The ARF Guidelines Handbook: A Compendium of Guidelines to Good Advertising, Marketing and Media Research Practice.*

Books on Media Content Analysis

Leinemann, Ralf, and Elena Baikaltseva. *Media Relations Measurement*. Aldershot, Hampshire, England: Gower, 2004.

Stacks, Don W. *Primer of Public Relations Research*. New York: Guilford Press, 2002.

REFERENCES FOR TRUST RESEARCH AND MEASUREMENT

Shockley-Zalabak, Pamela, Kathleen Ellis, and Ruggero Cesaria. *Measuring Organizational Trust: A Diagnostic Survey and International Indicator.* San Francisco: IABC Research Foundation, 2000.

From the IPR website, www.instituteforpr.org:

- *Can There Be Just One Trust? A Cross-Disciplinary Identification of Trust Definitions and Measurement* by Marcia Watson.
- *Guidelines for Measuring Relationships in Public Relations* by Linda Childers Hon and James E. Grunig.
- *Guidelines for Measuring Trust in Organizations* by Katie Paine, in association with Linda Hon and Jim Grunig.
- *Restoring Trust in Business: Models for Action* by The Public Relations Coalition.

WEBSITES

www.kdpaine.com KDPaine & Partners' company website and public relations measurement resource center; includes guides to vendors and many free papers.

www.themeasurementstandard.com KDPaine & Partners' monthly newsletter on public relations measurement.

http://kdpaine.blogs.com/ Katie Delahaye Paine's public relations measurement blog.

www.instituteforpr.org The site of the Institute for Public Relations; includes many free papers and resources.

http://sncr.org The site of the society for New Communications Research; includes many free papers and resources.

GLOSSARY

"Say, oh wise man, how have you come to such knowledge?"

"Because I was never ashamed to confess my ignorance and ask others."
—Johann Gottfried von Herder

A large part of measurement is about language. In fact (to use a concept adapted from John Gray's *Men Are from Mars, Women Are from Venus*, www.marsvenus.com), it is about the two different languages used by Martians and Venusians. Venusians are people who tend to think and speak in a style most readily expressed by words—words like messages, target audiences, and relationships. In the business world, Venusians tend to work in communications. Martians tend to think and speak in a style most readily expressed by numbers—numbers like ROI, revenue, and quarterly results. And in business, Martians tend to be in management. And so it often happens that Venusians have a difficult time communicating in a fashion that Martians can understand—and vice versa. One of the benefits of measurement is that it allows communications and management to talk to each other.

Over time, researchers and measurement experts have developed their own terms that can frequently be confusing to the person who is new to the measurement process. This Glossary has been adapted from the Dictionary of Public Relations Measurement and Research from the Commission on Public Relations Measurement and Evaluation, edited and compiled by Dr. Don Stacks of the University of Miami, and fully downloadable from the IPR's website, www.instituteforpr.org. Italic terms in the definitions indicate cross references.

Advertising value equivalent (AVE)   An unproven and suspect measure of PR value based on calculating the *column inches* of a story and determining the equivalent cost of buying the same size advertising space in the same publication.

Baseline or benchmark   An initial measurement against which subsequent measures are compared.

Benchmarking or benchmark study   A measurement technique that involves having an organization learn something about its own practices and/or the practices of selected others, and then compares these practices. Research that establishes a *benchmark*.

Causal relationship   A relationship between variables in which a change in one variable forces, produces, or brings about a change in another variable.

Census   A collection of data from every person or object in a population.

Circulation   Number of copies of a publication as distributed. Not usually the same as the number actually read, but as a practical matter, synonymous with *opportunities to see*, *impressions*, and *reach*.

Column inches   The total length of a printed article if it were all one column, measured in inches.

Communication(s) audit   A systematic review and analysis of how effectively an organization communicates with all of its major internal and external audiences.

Content analysis   An informal research methodology and measurement tool that systematically tracks messages (written, spoken, broadcast) and translates them into quantifiable form by defining message categories and specified units of analysis.

Correlation   A statistical test that examines the relationships between variables.

Cost per message communicated (CPMC)   Similar to *CPM*, but adjusted for the number of messages that actually appeared in the media coverage. Note that here "M" refers to "message."

Cost per thousand (CPM)   Cost per impression or cost per person reached. As used in advertising, it is the cost of advertising for each

1,000 homes reached. Note that here "M" refers to "thousand," as M is the Roman numeral for 1,000.

Dashboard   A technique for simplifying data reporting by displaying a small number of important summary measures together in one location. Like an automotive dashboard, a PR dashboard includes only those measures most critical for assessing the progress or health of a program or company.

Demographic analysis   The analysis of a population in terms of social, political, economic, and geographic subgroups (for example, age, sex, income level, race, educational level, place of residence, occupation).

Demographic data   Data that differentiates between groups of people by social, political, economic, and geographic characteristics.

Editorial or earned media   (1) The content of a publication written by a journalist, as distinct from advertising content, which is determined by an advertiser; (2) An article expressing the editorial policy of a publication on a matter of interest (also known as a "leader" or "leading article"); (3) Space in a publication bought by an advertiser that includes journalistic copy intended to make the reader think it originates from an independent source (also known as an "advertorial").

Focus group methodology   An informal research technique that uses a group discussion approach to gain an in-depth understanding of a client, object, or product; is not generalizable to other focus groups or populations.

Frequency   A descriptive statistic that represents the number of objects being counted (for example, number of advertisements, number of people who attend an event, number of media release pickups).

Gross rating points (GRP)   A measure most broadcast advertisers use to determine the extent to which their advertising messages have penetrated a specific audience. The GRP of a show or ad represents the percentage of the total audience who actually viewed it.

Impressions   Opportunities to see an article or message generated by the total audited circulation of a publication. For example, if the *Wall Street Journal* has an audited circulation of 1.5 million, one article in that paper generates 1.5 million impressions or opportunities to see the story. Two articles generate 3 million impressions, and so on. *Opportunities to see, circulation, impressions*, and *reach* are synonymous.

Key message   A specific statement or concept that an organization is trying to communicate about itself. A common general goal of PR is to get key messages into media coverage. A key message ought to be unique to your organization and it must be something that a journalist is likely to print, for example, "Company X provides the best customer service in the industry," or, "Company Y's product is of the highest quality."

Message content   (1) The verbal, visual, and audio elements of a message; (2) The material from which *content analyses* are conducted; (3) A *trend analysis* factor that measures what planned messages are actually contained in the media.

Message content analysis   Analysis of media coverage of a client, product, or topic on key issues.

Message strength   How strongly a message about a client, product, or topic was communicated.

Objectives   A clearly defined set of goals that are in line with overall strategic marketing, sales, and corporate objectives.

Omnibus survey   An all-purpose national consumer *poll* usually conducted on a regular schedule (once a week or every other week) by major market research firms; also called a "piggyback" or "shared-cost" *survey*.

Opportunities to see (OTS)   A number equal to the total audited circulation of a publication. *Opportunities to see, circulation, impressions*, and *reach* are synonymous.

Outcomes   Quantifiable changes in attitudes, behaviors, or opinions that occur as end results of a PR program.

Outputs   The physical products of a PR program; anything that is published or directly produced by the public relations team. Outputs can be articles, white papers, speaking engagements, the number of times a spokesperson is quoted, specific messages communicated, specific positioning on an important issue, or any number of quantifiable items.

Outtakes   What members of your target audiences take away from your program—the messages, perceptions, and understandings that your program has generated. *Outtakes* are the perceptions generated by your *outputs*.

Poll   (1) A form of *survey* research that focuses more on immediate behavior than attitudes; (2) A very short *survey*-like method using a *questionnaire* that asks only very short and closed-ended questions.

Positioning   How an organization is perceived on broad industry characteristics, such as leadership, innovation, employer of choice, neighbor of choice, and so forth.

Program or campaign   The planning, execution, and evaluation of a public relations plan of action aimed at solving a problem.

Psychographic research   Research focusing on nondemographic traits and characteristics such as personality type, lifestyle, social roles, values, attitudes, and beliefs.

Public   (1) A group of people whose behavior may have consequences for an organization or who are affected by the consequences of organizational decisions; (2) A group of people from which a public relations campaign or program selects specific *targeted audiences* in an attempt to influence behavior or attitudes regarding a company, product, issue, or individual.

Qualitative research   Studies that are somewhat to totally subjective, but nevertheless in-depth, using a probing, open-ended response format.

Quantitative research   Studies that are highly objective and projectable, using closed-ended, forced-choice *questionnaires;* research that relies heavily on statistics and numerical measures.

Questionnaire A measurement instrument that uses questions to collect data for the analysis of some aspect of a group. May be employed through the mail, Internet, in person, or via the telephone. May be both closed-ended and open-ended, but typically employs more closed-ended questions. A questionnaire is the instrument used in a *survey*.

Reach The scope or range of distribution and thus coverage that a given communication product has in a targeted audience group. The total audited *circulation* of a publication. In broadcasting, the net unduplicated (also called "deduplicated") radio or TV audience for programs. *Opportunities to see, circulation, impressions,* and *reach* are synonymous.

Reach demographics *Reach* into specific demographic segments, determined using data from one of the generally accepted sources such as SRDS or Simmons.

Response rate The number of respondents who actually complete an interview or reply to some request, usually expressed as a percentage of all those who received the interview or request.

Sample A group of people or objects chosen from a larger population.

Share of ink (SOI) The percentage of total press coverage or *opportunities to see* devoted to a particular client or product.

Share of voice (SOV) The percentage of total radio or television coverage or *opportunities to see* devoted to a particular client or product; also known as "share of coverage."

Survey The process of gathering data from a *sample* of a population. The instrument used in a survey is called a *questionnaire*.

Target audience A specific subset of a total audience, differentiated by some characteristic or attribute (for example, sports fishermen), that is the specific focus of a marketing or public relations effort.

Targeted gross rating points (TGRP) *Gross rating points* (GRP) with respect to a particular group or *target audience*.

Tone   Trend and *content analysis* factor that measures how a *target audience* feels about the client, product, or topic; typically defined as positive, neutral/balanced, or negative.

Trend analysis   Tracking of performance over the course of a PR campaign or program. A *survey* method whereby a topic or subject is examined over a period of time through repeated surveys of independently selected *samples*.

REFERENCES

Frankfurt, Henry G. 2005. *On bullshit*. Princeton, N.J.: Princeton University Press.

Gittell, R., and B. Gottlob B. 2001. *The economic impact of New Hampshire's first-in-the-nation primary*. Concord, NH: Library and Archives of New Hampshire's Political Tradition.

Grunig, J. E., and L. Hon. 1999. *Guidelines for measuring relationships in public relations*. Gainesville, FL: The Institute for Public Relations.

Grunig, J. E., and F. C. Repper, F. C. 1992. Strategic management, publics, and issues. In *Excellence in public relations and communication management*, ed. J. E. Grunig, 117–158. Hillsdale, NJ: Lawrence Erlbaum Associates.

Grunig, L. A., J. E. Grunig, and D. M. Dozier. 1992. *Public relations and effective organizations*. New York: Routledge.

Grunig, L. A., J. E. Grunig, and D. M. Dozier. *Excellent public relations and effective organizations: A study of communication management in three countries*. Mahwah, NJ: Lawrence Erlbaum Associates.

INDEX